THE LAYMAN'S BIBLE COMMENTARY

THE LAYMAN'S BIBLE COMMENTARY
IN TWENTY-FIVE VOLUMES

THE LAYMAN'S
BIBLE COMMENTARY

Balmer H. Kelly, *Editor*

Donald G. Miller   *Associate Editors*   Arnold B. Rhodes

Dwight M. Chalmers, *Editor, John Knox Press*

VOLUME 23

THE FIRST AND SECOND LETTERS OF PAUL TO THE
THESSALONIANS

THE FIRST AND SECOND LETTERS OF PAUL TO
TIMOTHY

THE LETTER OF PAUL TO
TITUS

THE LETTER OF PAUL TO
PHILEMON

Holmes Rolston

JOHN KNOX PRESS
RICHMOND, VIRGINIA

Published in Great Britain by SCM Press Ltd., London. Published simultaneously in Canada by The Ryerson Press, Toronto.

Third printing 1970

International Standard Book Number: 0-8042-3023-4
Library of Congress Card Number: 59-10454
Printed in the United States of America

PREFACE

The LAYMAN'S BIBLE COMMENTARY is based on the conviction that the Bible has the Word of good news for the whole world. The Bible is not the property of a special group. It is not even the property and concern of the Church alone. It is given to the Church for its own life but also to bring God's offer of life to all mankind—wherever there are ears to hear and hearts to respond.

It is this point of view which binds the separate parts of the LAYMAN'S BIBLE COMMENTARY into a unity. There are many volumes and many writers, coming from varied backgrounds, as is the case with the Bible itself. But also as with the Bible there is a unity of purpose and of faith. The purpose is to clarify the situations and language of the Bible that it may be more and more fully understood. The faith is that in the Bible there is essentially one Word, one message of salvation, one gospel.

The LAYMAN'S BIBLE COMMENTARY is designed to be a concise non-technical guide for the layman in personal study of his own Bible. Therefore, no biblical text is printed along with the comment upon it. This commentary will have done its work precisely to the degree in which it moves its readers to take up the Bible for themselves.

The writers have used the Revised Standard Version of the Bible as their basic text. Occasionally they have differed from this translation. Where this is the case they have given their reasons. In the main, no attempt has been made either to justify the wording of the Revised Standard Version or to compare it with other translations.

The objective in this commentary is to provide the most helpful explanation of fundamental matters in simple, up-to-date terms. Exhaustive treatment of subjects has not been undertaken.

In our age knowledge of the Bible is perilously low. At the same time there are signs that many people are longing for help in getting such knowledge. Knowledge of and about the Bible is, of course, not enough. The grace of God and the work of the Holy Spirit are essential to the renewal of life through the Scriptures. It is in the happy confidence that the great hunger for the Word is a sign of God's grace already operating within men, and that the Spirit works most wonderfully where the Word is familiarly known, that this commentary has been written and published.

THE EDITORS AND
THE PUBLISHERS

THESSALONIANS

———

INTRODUCTION

The Importance of the Thessalonian Letters

First and Second Thessalonians are among the most significant documents of the Christian Church. They were written to the church at Thessalonica by Paul while he was in the midst of his ministry at Corinth. Toward the close of his stay at Corinth, Paul was arrested and brought before Gallio, the proconsul of Achaia (Acts 18:12-17). By a study of some fragments of a Delphic inscription which were found in 1908, it is possible to fix with accuracy the coming of Gallio to Corinth in July of A.D. 51 or 52, with a strong probability for the earlier date. Since Paul had been in Corinth some time before he was brought before Gallio, the probability is that he reached Corinth early in A.D. 50 and that he wrote the Letters to the Thessalonians within a few months after his arrival. This would date these letters about A.D. 50. Even allowing for a small margin of error, we know with certainty that they were written about twenty years after the death of Christ. Many interpreters feel that Second Thessalonians was written only a few months later than First Thessalonians.

There are few things relating to Paul that have not been disputed at some time by someone. Objections have been raised to the Pauline authorship of both First and Second Thessalonians, and doubts have been raised concerning the genuineness of Second Thessalonians by some who acknowledge the first letter to be Pauline. It has been felt, for example, that the attitude taken toward the second coming of Christ in the second letter cannot be harmonized with the ideas expressed by Paul in First Thessalonians. But the overwhelming majority of informed opinion regards both letters as written by Paul. They were listed as letters of Paul and quoted as Pauline by the earliest Christian writers. And they are so intimately personal and so obviously written to a particular situation that they impress the average reader as undoubtedly genuine.

These letters probably carry us closer to the time of Christ than any other written documents which have come to us in unaltered form. It is to be assumed, of course, that much of the material which we now have in the four Gospels was written down before A.D. 50. Matthew, for example, may have kept a collection of the sayings of Jesus which went back to the days of his flesh. But the source material concerning the life of Jesus which was available in A.D. 50 was collected and edited at a later date. In fact, it was the existence of churches like the church in Thessalonica, in which followers of Jesus were seeking to imitate his way of life, that made it necessary for the Church to commit to writing its memory of the words and deeds of the Lord.

The Letters to the Thessalonians should not be considered in isolation from the other letters of Paul. For example, Paul wrote to the Thessalonians of the salvation received "through our Lord Jesus Christ, who died for us . . ." (I Thess. 5:9-10) at approximately the same time in his ministry that he wrote the Letter to the Galatians. Galatians contains a much fuller statement of the way in which Paul understood the significance of the death of Christ, a statement which may be used to enrich his meaning in Thessalonians, and when Paul, in writing to the Thessalonians concerning the Christian hope for those who have fallen asleep, says, "We believe that Jesus died and rose again" (I Thess. 4:14), we can be sure that in his ministry at Thessalonica he had given the witness to the Resurrection which he so clearly sets forth in the first part of the fifteenth chapter of First Corinthians. We can also assume that the summary of the characteristics of the Christian life which we find in I Thessalonians 5:14-22 is to be supplemented by the fuller treatment of this subject in the twelfth chapter of Romans.

While they are not to be considered in isolation from his other letters, the Letters to the Thessalonians are priceless in themselves because they reveal the mind and heart of Paul as an active missionary who, in co-operation with his companions Timothy and Silas, was laying the foundations of the Christian Church in Macedonia and Achaia about twenty years after the death of Christ. But valuable as these documents are for the knowledge of the thought of Paul at this stage of his life, they are much more valuable for the information which they give concerning what may properly be called primitive Christianity. We have here documents reflecting the life of the Christian church at Thessalonica less than twenty years after the first disciples went forth to give their witness to the resurrection of their Lord. These letters, then, give us our first direct look at a believing community which is functioning as a Christian church in the secular society of Greece about A.D. 50. It is not that this church at Thessalonica was a perfect community which Christians are to emulate in every respect today. Paul's letters leave us under no illusions as to the shortcomings of the churches which he founded. It would be strange indeed if a small body of early Christians, all of whom had come recently from Judaism or paganism, should set the ideal example of what a Christian church should be. But Christians today are tremendously interested in knowing the thoughts and emotions of those who stood very close to the time when the Lord was present in the flesh. Certainly many of the things which Paul said to the Christians at Thessalonica can become in a somewhat altered form the word of the Lord to his Church today.

The History of the Church at Thessalonica

In Acts 17:1-9 there is a brief description of Paul's ministry at Thessalonica. Paul, Silas, and Timothy came to Thessalonica as their first major stop after they had been driven from Philippi. First Thessalonians 2:2 refers to the knowledge which the readers had of the shameful treatment which Paul and his party had received at Philippi. Thessalonica is therefore the second city of Macedonia in which Paul made a prolonged effort to lay the foundations of a Christian church. There was a synagogue of the Jews at Thessalonica and Paul, in accordance with his custom, began his work by preaching in this synagogue. Over a period of three weeks he spoke to the Jews, explaining to them from their Scriptures the necessity for the suffering and death of the Christ. This was a central point of approach to the Jews, since the death of the Christ was to them from the beginning a major stumbling block in their acceptance of Christianity. The burden of Paul's message to the Jews was that the Jesus whom he proclaimed to them was the Christ. Paul won some converts among the Jews of Thessalonica, but in time he was driven from the synagogue. The passage in Acts taken by itself might lead to the conclusion that Paul and his party stayed for only a few weeks in Thessalonica, but the implications of his letters would suggest a longer period. We should notice also that in writing to the Philippians, Paul reminds them that during his stay at Thessalonica they sent him help at least twice (Phil. 4:15-16). This suggests a stay of some duration. The probability is that some time elapsed between Paul's leaving the synagogue and the organization of a mob by the Jews to drive the evangelists out of the city. During this time there were added to the church at Thessalonica "a great many of the devout Greeks and not a few of the leading women" (Acts 17:4). We have no way of knowing the total membership of this church. The letters point to a church that was active and growing. At best, however, the Christians were a small minority of believers, struggling to maintain their faith in the midst of a hostile environment.

Paul and Silas (and we would suppose Timothy also) were sent away from Thessalonica by the brethren to avoid further violence after a mob which failed to find Paul had dragged a member of the church named Jason before the city authorities. The cries of the mob indicate something of the nature of the charges against Paul (Acts 17:6-7). He and his companions were accused of turning the world upside down. Like many other charges made in hate, this accusation had in it some of the elements of a compliment. It points to the intense activity of the Christians and also to the reversal of accepted customs in a Christian community in which Jews and Gentiles mingled on terms of complete equality. The people of the mob said also that the Christians were acting against the decrees of Caesar in "saying that there is another king, Jesus" (Acts 17:7). This charge suggests the lines along which the Christians were later to be persecuted, as owing to Jesus an allegiance which conflicted with their loyalty to Caesar. But the conflict between the Christian Church and the Roman state had not developed at this time. In Paul's defense of his ministry in I Thessalonians 2:1-12, we may have his answer to an accusation that he had fled Thessalonica when persecution developed and had left his converts to suffer alone. We learn from Paul's letters that the Christians at Thessalonica continued to be persecuted by their own countrymen (I Thess. 2:14).

Paul and Silas went from Thessalonica to Beroea. In time the Jews from Thessalonica followed him to Beroea and sought to incite the crowds there against him. The determined nature of the opposition of the Jews to Paul at this time explains the force of his condemnation of them in I Thessalonians 2:14-16.

From Beroea, Paul went to Athens. The third chapter of First Thessalonians indicates that while he was at Athens, Paul became so concerned about the condition of the church at Thessalonica that he sent Timothy there to strengthen the church and to bring to him at Corinth a report concerning its spiritual condition.

The Occasion of the Thessalonian Letters

First Thessalonians was written by Paul to justify his ministry in Thessalonica in the light of the accusations that had been made against him and to comfort and strengthen a church which he knew was experiencing tribulation and persecution. Paul had recently received from Timothy a full report of conditions in this church. In his comments concerning the love of the brethren, in his warning against idleness, in his teachings concerning those who have fallen asleep, and in his comments concerning the times and the seasons in connection with the coming of "the day of the Lord," Paul was probably speaking to specific conditions as they had been reported to him by Timothy.

Second Thessalonians follows a movement somewhat similar to that of First Thessalonians. In this letter Paul repeats, with variations, many of the ideas which he has already expressed in the first epistle. We have, for example, in an expanded form his warnings against idleness (II Thess. 3:6-12). But the specific occasion for the letter was an increase in the intensity of the persecution of his converts and the exaggerated expectation of the near return of Christ which had led some people to say that it was useless to work or to engage in long-range planning. To meet this situation, Paul used the language of Jewish eschatology to point out some things which must take place before the return.

In their literary form First and Second Thessalonians are informal letters from a missionary to a church which he loves. At times Paul assumes information which he knows is common to him and his readers. Unfortunately those who read the letters today do not have the information which Paul assumes. Because of this, it is not possible in some cases to know his meaning with certainty. Personal letters are informal. A writer passes rapidly from one subject to another and does not hesitate to deal with the same subject in several different places. If we are to get the full teachings of the letters on any one subject, we have to glean carefully and collect the different sayings and organize them so that we may get the complete impact of what Paul has said. This is true in dealing with almost every major thrust of the epistles. But intimate personal letters are most revealing, for they open up the heart of the writer and the spiritual condition of those to whom he is writing.

The Message of the Thessalonian Letters

The expectation of the near return of the Lord permeates both Thessalonian letters. These Christians were close to the great events connected with the life and death and resurrection of Jesus Christ. They were waiting and longing for his return in glory and power, to bring to an end the present world order and set up the Kingdom of God. It is clear that the Thessalonians got this expectation of the near return of the Lord from Paul and his companions. It is clear also that Paul in these letters struggles with the abuse of the Christian hope of the return of Christ, and that there were elements in his thinking and in the understanding of the faith among his converts which would enable Christianity to survive the delay in the return of the Christ and to remain through the centuries a vital and dynamic faith.

The most frequently quoted verses from these letters are I Thessalonians 4:13-15. They are included in most of our funeral services. In them Paul declares, on the basis of a word of the Lord, that those who are asleep and those who are alive at the coming of Christ will be united and will share alike in the ultimate glories of the Kingdom of God. The most controversial passage in the letters is the description of the "man of lawlessness" in II Thessalonians 2:1-12, written originally in order to assure the Thessalonians that the coming of the Lord was not immediately at hand.

Paul's plea for the purity of family life in I Thessalonians 4:1-8 is a remarkable illustration of the way in which from the beginning, Christianity lifted the pagan world to a better understanding of sex. It is part also of the larger ethical message of the epistles, which does not deal with conduct in terms of moralism or legalism but insists that Christians should live in a manner that is worthy of their high calling as children of God.

The understanding of the person and work of Christ which underlies these letters is interesting as a revelation of the accepted faith of the Christian community within two decades of the time of Christ. There is a clear statement of the death of Jesus at the hands of his enemies. This is combined with the certainty of his resurrection and exaltation and the confident hope of his final manifestation in glory (I Thess. 1:10).

Paul's intensely practical considerations are shown in his effort to build at Thessalonica a brotherhood of those who loved each other and in his determination that the Christians should not find in their faith an excuse for idleness. In these and in other areas of faith and life Paul's advice to the Thessalonians has a vital message for Christians today.

OUTLINE

First Thessalonians

Second Thessalonians

COMMENTARY

THE COMING OF THE GOSPEL
TO THESSALONICA

I Thessalonians 1:1—2:16

The Church at Thessalonica (1:1-10)

The Letter to the Thessalonians is written by Paul, but he includes his companions, Silas and Timothy, in the sending of the letter. It was with the help of these men that Paul had carried the gospel to Thessalonica. In the letter as a whole he consistently writes in the first person plural as spokesman for the three evangelists. The man who is called Silvanus here is to be identified with the Silas of Acts (Acts 17:4). The Book of Acts pictures him as one of the leaders of the church at Jerusalem who were sent with Paul to Antioch after the Jerusalem Council to confirm by personal testimony the decree of this council (Acts 15:22). Paul chose him as his companion for the second missionary journey after his separation from Barnabas over the question of taking John Mark with them (Acts 15:36-41). Silas was with Paul in prison at Philippi and with him during the whole of his stay at Thessalonica. Timothy was one of Paul's converts during the first missionary journey. At Lystra, on the second missionary journey, Paul chose him to be an attendant (Acts 16:1-3). When Paul writes this letter from Corinth, Timothy has just returned from a mission to Thessalonica and Silas has also joined him.

The letter is addressed to the church of the Thessalonians. The Greek word for "church" which Paul used had not at this time acquired the specialized meaning it was later to have. It could have referred to any assembly of Thessalonians. Paul adds therefore that his letter is directed to the Thessalonians who acknowledge God as Father and Jesus Christ as Lord. The greetings of "grace" and "peace" are common to all his epistles. Grace points to the unmerited favor of God and peace to the acceptance with God which comes through Jesus Christ.

The letter opens with an expression of thanksgiving to God for the Thessalonian Christians. Paul declares that he constantly

mentions them in his prayers. In this, as in similar expressions
to other churches, we are given some idea of the place of inter-
cessory prayer in the life of Paul. As Paul prays for these Christians he remembers their work of faith, their labor of love, and
their steadfastness of hope in the Lord Jesus Christ (vs. 3). The
expressions are suggestive. They point to a faith that has issued
in works, to labors that have been inspired by love, and to a
hope in the Lord Jesus Christ which has proved steadfast in the
time of testing.

Paul's memory of the Thessalonian Christians leads him to a
description of the characteristics of this church, which covers the
rest of the first chapter. The Thessalonians are beloved of God
and God has chosen them. This idea is central to Paul's concept
of the Church. The believers at Thessalonica are those whom
God has called into the fellowship of his Church. The root idea
of the Greek word for "church" points to an assembly of those
who have been called from the larger secular community into a
believing fellowship. The call has been given through the proclamation of the gospel. And in the mystery of proclamation and
response God has called this Church into being.

The gospel has come to Thessalonica "not only in word, but
also in power and in the Holy Spirit and with full conviction"
(vs. 5). As Paul and his companions have preached the gospel
in Thessalonica, God has honored their preaching by calling men
and women to become his followers. The proclamation of the
word has had in it a dynamic element. Beyond the human word
there has been God's act. Moreover, the Holy Spirit has brought
to the Thessalonians an inner conviction of the truth of the gospel message.

The Thessalonians have received the word in "much affliction" but also with a "joy inspired by the Holy Spirit" (vs. 6).
This is the first reference to the afflictions which the Thessalonians have had to suffer. As followers of Jesus, they have
sought to imitate the way of life which they saw first in the
lives of Paul, Silas, and Timothy, and then through them in
the life of Jesus himself. This necessitated their receiving from
Paul and his companions some instruction in the words and
deeds of Jesus.

In their effort to follow the way of Jesus as they had seen it
set forth in the life of Paul, the Thessalonians became faithful
Christians. The life of the believers at Thessalonica became "an

example to all the believers in Macedonia and in Achaia" (vs. 7). Through their way of life and through their proclamation of the gospel to others the Thessalonian Christians became a witnessing community, their faith known throughout the whole Church. Christians who came to Paul at Corinth from various sections of the Church commented to him concerning the remarkable results of his work at Thessalonica.

Those who were now members of the church had "turned to God from idols, to serve a living and true God" (vs. 9). This statement would suggest that a majority of the members of this church were of Gentile background, for the Jews would not have come to Christianity from idolatry. The Greeks of the first century were worshipers of idols. Even in Athens, the center of Greek culture, Paul's "spirit was provoked within him as he saw that the city was full of idols" (Acts 17:16). In contrast to the gods of the pagan world, the God whom Paul worshiped was the true God. The pagan gods were deifications of the lusts of men and creations of the minds of men. They had no actual existence. But the God who makes himself known to us in Jesus Christ is the true God. He is also the living God, the God who acts. He has revealed himself in that he has raised Jesus from the dead.

In these verses, Paul describes some great convictions which the Thessalonian Christians had accepted as they turned from the worship of idols to the service of the true and living God. He refers to Jesus as God's Son. While using the human name "Jesus," Paul insists that this person, who had lived in Palestine about twenty years before, is to be recognized in a unique sense as the Son of God. This is the conviction at the heart of the faith of the Christian community in the earliest Christian document that we have. The Thessalonians had accepted the witness which Paul and his companions had given to the resurrection of Jesus from the dead. They believed that this Jesus who had come from the Father had returned to the Father. This points to the Christian doctrine of the ascension of Jesus. The early Christians believed that their crucified and risen Lord was seated at the right hand of the Father in glory and in power. This was their way of saying that the Son was with the Father as Lord of the universe.

These Christians were waiting for the return of the Jesus who had been raised from the dead and who had ascended to the Father (vs. 10). We strike here the most characteristic note of the Letters to the Thessalonians. The early Christians were watching and longing for the return of the Lord. And the Letters to the Thessalonians are dominated by the expectancy of the near return of Christ. This is not surprising. The early Christians stood close to Jesus. They had received from him a tremendous sense of the reality of the unseen world of God. Many of those at Jerusalem, including perhaps Silas, had been among the ones to whom Jesus had "presented himself alive after his passion by many proofs, appearing to them during forty days, and speaking of the kingdom of God" (Acts 1:3). In any case, we can be certain that Silas knew intimately some of those to whom Jesus had revealed himself alive after his Passion. Paul himself had seen the Risen Lord (I Cor. 9:1; 15:8; Acts 9:5; 22:8; 26:15). This manifestation of the Lord gave to the early Christians an assured knowledge of the world of the resurrection which the Risen Lord had revealed. It is natural that they should have hoped for a culmination of history in the full disclosure of this world which had been opened up to them by his resurrection. As the events of history have demonstrated, the early Christians were wrong in their expectancy of an immediate return of Christ. They were right in seeing all of our human life in the light of the reality of the Resurrection.

They were also right in their belief that it is Jesus who delivers us from the wrath to come. The salvation which Jesus brought to the Thessalonian Christians was not a trivial thing. It included forgiveness of sins, acceptance with God, and deliverance from the fear of judgment to come. Christians today still believe in a consummation of history in the final disclosure of the reality of the world to which Jesus has gone. And Christians today feel that in the certainty of death, the individual faces the same necessity for being ready to meet the Lord that the early Christians found in their expectation of the near return of the Lord from heaven. Whether we are alive at the time of his coming or whether we must face death before he comes, we must all appear before the judgment seat of Christ (II Cor. 5:10). And Christians today, as the Christians at Thessalonica, look to Jesus as the One "who delivers us from the wrath to come" (vs. 10).

Paul's Ministry at Thessalonica (2:1-12)

Paul next turns to a defense of his ministry at Thessalonica.

He writes as a man whose conduct has been under attack. He had many enemies, since his proclamation of the gospel always aroused opposition. It may be that his enemies were accusing him of being a shepherd who had left his flock at the first sign of danger. We know from his letter that after his departure the Christians at Thessalonica continued to face severe persecutions. His enemies may have asserted that he was afraid to return to Thessalonica. It is clear, of course, that Paul left on the insistence of the brethren at Thessalonica, who were concerned for his protection and wished to avoid another mob demonstration (Acts 17:10). But his sudden departure was obviously open to misinterpretation. It is against a background such as this that Paul gave a full picture of the ministry which he and his companions carried on in Thessalonica. In so doing, he penned one of the richest descriptions of the work of a Christian minister to be found in the New Testament. The Thessalonians knew that Paul and his companions had come to them after shameful treatment at Philippi. But the evangelists did not let their experiences at Philippi keep them from preaching the gospel with courage at Thessalonica. As was to be expected, they met with strong opposition, but they persisted in their proclamation of the gospel.

In his preaching, Paul resisted all temptations to tone down the message of the gospel so as to rob it of the element of offense. Most of the great idolatries are attractive to their adherents because they deify and sanctify the lusts of men. The worship of the Greek gods called for little discipline of the passions of their devotees. Paul spoke as a man who was free from guile. He did not present a sugar-coated gospel (2:3).

Deep in Paul's consciousness was the knowledge that he had been called by God to be the Apostle to the Gentiles. He speaks of himself here as one "approved by God to be entrusted with the gospel" (2:4). He knew, therefore, that his first obligation was to be faithful to his message and to seek to please the God who had sent him. This concern to please God delivered him from the subtle temptation of preaching to please men. Paul was not unconcerned, however, as to what the Thessalonians thought of his ministry. The whole thrust of the passage is an effort to commend his ministry to his Thessalonian converts and to present himself to them as a minister of Christ who deserves their complete confidence. The tenderness which pervades this whole passage reveals a minister who is deeply concerned to win the love of his people. He is filled with joy when Timothy reports that the Thessalonians remember him kindly and long to see him (3:6). Paul's sense of his responsibility to God and his desire to be worthy of the genuine affection of his people saved him from the temptation to deal in flattery or to seek glory from men.

Paul insists that he has not used the preaching of the gospel as a cloak for greed. In another connection he defends the right of the minister to receive his support from those to whom he ministers (I Cor. 9:1-19; see also I Tim. 5:17-18). He knows that the Lord has "commanded that those who proclaim the gospel should get their living by the gospel" (I Cor. 9:14). He has no objection to receiving, while at Thessalonica, offerings from the church which he has recently established at Philippi (Phil. 4:16). He knows that as an Apostle he has the right to ask help from the Thessalonians, but he has not used this right because he is anxious to be free from all suspicion of preaching for money.

In his ministry at Thessalonica, Paul was as gentle as a nurse taking care of her children (vs. 7). A dwarf trying to carry a wounded man over a river will worsen his wounds, while a giant can carry such a man across easily without hurting him. Paul knew the tenderness that is possible only to strength.

The true minister must give himself as he seeks to share the gospel of God with others. During his time in Thessalonica, Paul had given himself completely to his ministry to the people there. He had laid down a portion of his life, and the Thessalonians had become very dear to him (vs. 8).

Since they did not receive support from the Thessalonian Christians, it was necessary for Paul, Silas, and Timothy to support themselves by their own labor (vs. 9). They received some help in the form of gifts from the Philippians, but these gifts must have been inadequate for their full support. It was necessary, therefore, for the evangelists to find some form of gainful occupation and to labor night and day to make a living in order that they might not be a burden to any of the Thessalonians. Apparently Paul worked at his trade of tentmaking. Thus he set for the Thessalonians an example of industry which some of them sorely needed, while at the same time he maintained his independence. It must be remembered, however, that a modern church, with its complicated program of activities, cannot afford to have its pastor give a major portion of his time to worldly cares and avocations. Paul clearly established the right of a minister to receive the support that he needs in order that he may give himself without reservation to his task.

In describing his pastoral care of his people, Paul likens himself to a father with his children (vss. 10-11). He calls God and the Thessalonians to witness to the way in which he has been holy, righteous, and blameless in his ministry to the believers at Thessalonica. This is the picture of a man of God who loves his spiritual children as if they were his children according to the flesh, and who goes among them encouraging each one as he seeks to lead a Christian life. The description of his work at Thessalonica is similar to the picture which Paul paints of his work at Ephesus (Acts 20:20-21).

In bringing this subject to a close Paul writes: "We . . . charged you to lead a life worthy of God, who calls you into his own kingdom and glory" (vss. 11-12). Look first at the final clause of verse 12. The call has come through Paul's proclamation of the gospel. The church at Thessalonica is made up of those who have heard this call and responded to it. They have been laid hold of by an eternal salvation. Their place in the Kingdom of God is in part a fact of the present. They have acknowledged Jesus as Lord; they have turned from the worship of idols to serve the true and living God; they are seeking to imitate the pattern of life which Jesus has set for them; they are looking to Jesus for deliverance from the wrath to come. The participation of these Christians in the Kingdom of God, however, belongs in part to the future. The full consummation of the call into God's glory lies in the future.

But Paul's thought in this passage is centered not on the call but on the life which men should lead when they have received this call. Christians must live in a way that is worthy of their calling. They must live in a manner that is pleasing to the God who has called them. In their life on earth they must bear witness to the fact that their citizenship is in heaven (Phil. 3:20). Here is the true basis of Christian ethics. Paul had reacted violently against the legalism of Judaism. He knew that men could not be saved by keeping the Law. He would react with equal violence against moralism, against an attempt to understand the Christian life in terms of a moral code that is not grounded in Christian theology. He would not have understood Christianity in terms of trying to live up to the ideals set forth in the Sermon on the Mount. And he would have been equally opposed to any form of lawlessness in which every Christian thought that he could do as he pleased. Instead, Paul reminds Christians that God has called them into his own Kingdom and glory, and he tells them that they must live in a way that is worthy of the God who calls them.

The Acceptance of Paul's Message (2:13-16)

Deeper than his concern for himself is Paul's concern that his message be accepted as true. He constantly gives thanks to God for the way in which the gospel was received in Thessalonica. The Thessalonians had received his message, not as the word of men, but as what it really was, the word of God. In the Letter to the Galatians (which was probably written about the same time as this Letter to the Thessalonians), Paul makes it very clear that the gospel which he preached was not his own invention, but that he received it "through a revelation of Jesus Christ" (Gal. 1:11-12). In the same letter he insists that he has received his apostleship by divine appointment (Gal. 1:1). These statements are not to be interpreted to mean that Paul did not learn many of the facts connected with the life of Jesus from those who had known Jesus during his public ministry. His close associations with Barnabas and Silas are sufficient to establish the intimate nature of his contact with the beginnings of Christianity at Jerusalem. And Paul remarks in Galatians that he spent fifteen days with Peter in Jerusalem. He knew also James, the Lord's brother (Gal. 1:19), and John, the Apostle (Gal. 2:9). He was sure that the gospel he preached was not out of harmony with the message proclaimed by Peter, James, and John, but he was very certain that the gospel he preached was not a human invention. He was sent to the Gentiles to bear witness to God's revelation of himself in Jesus Christ. He went as the spokesman for God, and the message which he proclaimed was God's message of salvation to sinful men.

In Thessalonians, however, Paul is not primarily concerned to assert the divine origin of his message. His stress here is on the fact that the Thessalonians had accepted his message as the word of God. It is somewhat amazing that three men who had been driven out of Philippi could come to Thessalonica without any external authentication and persuade a considerable number of people that they were the bearers of the word of God. This is particularly difficult to understand when it is clear that the acceptance of this message involved, on the part of those who received it, strenuous obligations associated with a new way of life. It also involved membership in a community which was despised and persecuted. From the beginning the Thessalonians "received the word in much affliction" (1:6).

An explanation of the acceptance of Paul's message as the word of God by many of the Thessalonians is to be found in the intensity with which Paul, Silas, and Timothy believed that they were the bearers of God's offer of salvation. The evangelists endured hardships and supported themselves by their own labors in order that they might have the opportunity of preaching at Thessalonica. Unless men hold to their convictions with great intensity they are not apt to communicate their faith effectively to others. The man who feels that "there are few things worth living for and none worth dying for" will not gather around himself a band of zealous disciples. But no amount of emphasis on the intensity with which Paul held his beliefs can fully explain the way in which his message was received as the word of God by the Thessalonians. The explanation has been given in chapter 1, where Paul insists that the acceptance of his gospel was due to the work of the Holy Spirit in the hearts of those who heard him (1:5). He states the same thing in a somewhat different fashion when he says that the calling into being of the Thessalonian church was an act of God (2:12).

The reference to "the churches . . . in Judea" points to persecutions which took place before A.D. 50. We cannot identify these persecutions with accuracy. They may be ones such as Paul himself earlier had led in an effort to stamp out Christianity, or they may be others unknown to us. In either case, the Christians at Thessalonica became imitators of the churches in Judea in that they suffered from their own countrymen the same things that the Christians in Judea had suffered from the Jews. The mob which forced Paul to leave Thessalonica had been incited by the Jews. But evidently the Thessalonians at a later time had suffered persecutions from their own countrymen, that is, the Greeks.

Why was it that the Christian communities founded by Paul became almost immediately the object of persecutions from their pagan neighbors? The evangelists preached a gospel which made total demands on men. They preached an intolerant faith which branded the worship of the Greek and Roman gods as idolatry, as the worship of gods which had no real existence. When men received this faith, a line of division came between them and their unbelieving neighbors. Jesus himself had fully foreseen the effect of the proclamation of the gospel in a pagan world (see, for example, Matt. 10:34-38; Luke 12:49-51). Jesus has properly been called the Great Disturber. The great conceptions which were involved in the gospel could not be accepted as the word of God, apart from strife and division. Paul and Silas were described in Thessalonica as belonging to those who were turning the world upside down. Later Paul was to write to Timothy: "Indeed all who desire to live a godly life in Christ Jesus will be persecuted" (II Tim. 3:12). When the Thessalonians accepted Paul's message as the word of God and sought to order their lives in obedience to the demands of the gospel, they were certain in time to arouse the opposition of their own countrymen.

The description of the Jews in I Thessalonians 2:15-16 could be left out without breaking at all the movement of Paul's thought in this letter. Having mentioned the Jews, Paul's mind goes off at a tangent. In a priceless aside, which is not relevant to his thought but is intensely interesting, he says that the Jews killed the Lord Jesus. It is a matter of historical interest that in this document, which goes back to within twenty years of the death of Jesus, Paul places the responsibility for the death of Jesus squarely upon the Jews. This, of course, does not contradict another statement in which he says that "the rulers of this age" crucified the Lord of glory (I Cor. 2:8). The execution of Jesus was carried out by the Romans, Pontius Pilate and Herod Antipas sharing in the responsibility. But the moving spirit in bringing about the death of Jesus was the attitude of some of the Jewish leaders to him.

Some commentators have thought that Paul shows a strange sense of anticlimax when he says: "the Jews . . . killed both the Lord Jesus and the prophets, and drove us out" (2:14-15). Surely we would expect him to list the death of the Christ as the culmination of Israel's sin. But the death of Jesus is not seen as an isolated act by a few leaders of the Jews. Instead Paul sees it as an expression of an abiding attitude, as part of a pattern. In the past the Jews have killed their prophets. They have also killed the Lord Jesus, and now they have driven Paul out. Jews in Thes-

salonica were responsible for the mob action which forced Paul
to flee to Beroea, and the same Jewish leaders followed him
there, making it necessary for him to leave that city in haste for
Athens. And even as Paul writes in Corinth, tensions are building up which will lead to the scene in which the Jews bring him
before the tribunal of Gallio. In Thessalonica, Paul does not face
the Judaizers. The Judaizers were Jewish Christians who sought
to bind circumcision and the keeping of the Law of Moses on
the churches of Galatia as conditions of salvation. The red-hot
Letter to the Galatians is Paul's answer to this distortion of his
gospel. The Letters to the Thessalonians give no indication of the
presence of Judaizers in Thessalonica. In Thessalonica, Paul is
facing Jews who had rejected his gospel and were attempting to
crush the Christian movement before it could become rooted in
the Gentile world.

In continuing his indictment of these Jews, Paul declares that
they "displease God and oppose all men by hindering us from
speaking to the Gentiles that they may be saved" (2:15-16). If
the Jews had succeeded, the Gentiles would not have received
the message of the gospel and the Gentile members of the church
at Thessalonica would not have been saved. And these Gentile
Christians at Thessalonica were merely a token of the millions
of Gentiles who would find their way into the Kingdom of God.
The insistence that the cup of the iniquity of the Jews is almost
full is not a prediction of the fall of Jerusalem which was to take
place about twenty years later. It is simply Paul's understanding
of the way in which sin that is persisted in brings judgment. Of
course, Paul spoke of certain Jews at a particular time in history.
But there is a sense in which the Israel which has persisted in the
rejection of Jesus as the Christ shares in the guilt of the Jews of
the time of Paul. There is no note of tenderness in this comment
on the Jews of his time, but it is only one of the statements of
Paul. A few years later he could write: "I have great sorrow and
unceasing anguish in my heart. For I could wish that I myself
were accursed and cut off from Christ for the sake of my brethren, my kinsmen by race. . . . Brethren, my heart's desire and
prayer to God for them is that they may be saved" (Romans
9:2-3; 10:1).

THE MISSION OF TIMOTHY

I Thessalonians 2:17—3:13

Paul's Desire to Return to Thessalonica (2:17-20)

Here Paul returns to his theme. He assures the Thessalonians that it had been his intention to visit them again. The intensity with which Paul insists that this has been his purpose suggests that he is under attack at this point. His enemies may have suggested that he had fled at the first sign of persecution and had left his followers to bear alone the brunt of the persecution. The passage as a whole is a remarkable revelation of the love which Paul felt for his followers at Thessalonica. He insists that when he left Thessalonica he had every intention of returning, but he could not come to them because Satan hindered him. Paul believed in a personal Devil and felt that the things which had prevented his return were part of the activity of Satan.

In a vivid figure (vs. 19) Paul sees himself as presenting the Thessalonian Christians to the Lord Jesus on his return as the fruit of the ministry which he and Silas and Timothy had carried on in Thessalonica. If Jesus returned during Paul's lifetime, Paul did not expect to greet him empty-handed. Instead, as the crown of his boasting before the Lord, Paul intended to present to him the persons won at Thessalonica. The second coming of Jesus is definitely in Paul's mind here. But the idea can be applied with equal force to the Christian's meeting with Jesus at death. The evangelists at Thessalonica had had the high privilege of seeing a Christian church called into being through their witness to Jesus Christ. They expected to be able to point to these Christians as their glory and joy when they had to give an account to their Lord of the deeds done in the flesh.

The Mission of Timothy (3:1-5)

Since it had not proved possible for Paul to return to Thessalonica, he had decided to send Timothy as his representative. According to the narrative in Acts, when trouble arose at Beroea the brethren there conducted Paul to Athens, while Silas and Timothy remained at Beroea. Paul sent word by the brethren directing Silas and Timothy to join him at once in Athens (Acts 17:14-15). If we had to depend on the narrative of Acts alone, we would assume that they did not reach Paul until after he had been for some time at Corinth (Acts 18:1-5). But it seems clear from this letter that Timothy did come to Paul in Athens. Paul at that time had evidently heard reports of the persecutions at Thessalonica, which deeply disturbed him. He yearned to have Timothy with him, for he felt very much alone in Athens, but he had decided that he must send him back to Thessalonica. In this passage Paul commends Timothy as "our brother and God's servant in the gospel of Christ." (See also the beautiful tribute to Timothy in Philippians 2:19-24.) Timothy was sent to establish the Thessalonians in the faith and to comfort them so that no one would deny the faith on account of afflictions. The sending of Timothy was therefore another indication of the intensity of the persecution which the Christians in Thessalonica were facing.

In the effort to nerve the Thessalonians to remain steadfast in the midst of these continuing persecutions, Paul reminds them of the instructions he had given to them while he was with them. He had told them that as members of the Christian Church they could expect to suffer afflictions. His reference may be in part to the experiences of suffering which are the common lot of humanity. But the setting of the passage would indicate that he is referring primarily to the peculiar difficulties which they face as Christians in the midst of a secular society which acknowledges a different set of values. In a similar message to the Christians at Lystra and Iconium he has spoken "strengthening the souls of the disciples, exhorting them to continue in the faith, and saying that through many tribulations we must enter the kingdom of God" (Acts 14:22). Paul had invited the Thessalonians to join the Church militant, not the Church triumphant. He had made it clear to them that as good soldiers of Jesus Christ they must be prepared to suffer afflictions, and his words had proved true in their experience.

The Report of Timothy (3:6-10)

The First Letter to the Thessalonians was written after Timothy had returned from his visit and had given a good report of the spiritual condition of the Thessalonian church. This would date the letter near the beginning of Paul's ministry in Corinth. The report of Timothy was most encouraging, for he brought to Paul good news of the faith and love of his converts. He reported that the Thessalonians remembered Paul kindly and longed to see him. Probably a major motivation to these new Christians in their effort to be faithful to Christ in all circumstances was the knowledge of Paul's concern for them. One can face the day of temptation when he has a trusted friend who believes in him and loves him. After he had received Timothy's report, Paul poured out his heart in thanksgiving to God for the joy which had come to him because of the fidelity of his Christian friends at Thessalonica. He still expressed the hope that he might be permitted to visit them to strengthen that which was lacking in their faith.

A Prayer for the Thessalonian Christians (3:11-13)

The movement of the First Letter to the Thessalonians comes to an appropriate stopping point at the close of the third chapter. In an intensely personal letter, Paul has described the coming of the gospel to the Thessalonians. He has defended his ministry among them and explained his failure to return to them. He has sent Timothy to strengthen them in time of persecution and has expressed his joy at the good news from them which Timothy has brought. He now closes this portion of the letter with a prayer. The first petition is that God the Father and the Lord Jesus will direct his way to them. As far as we know, this prayer did not receive an immediate answer. Complete information about the movements of Paul is not available. But as far as is known he did not get back to Thessalonica until he passed through Macedonia and Greece on his final trip to Jerusalem. At this time, Aristarchus and Secundus of Thessalonica joined his party and went with him to Rome (Acts 20:1-5).

Verse 12 and 4:9-10 describe the church at Thessalonica as a community of love. The request is that the Lord will make them abound and increase in love. Christian love is the result of the work of Christ in the heart of the believer. The Thessalonians had already made progress in constituting a community of love. But they are not to be satisfied with their attainments; they must increase and abound in love. This love is first of all their love for one another. The place for Christian love to begin is in the inner life of the local church. The cement of the Christian fellowship is love. But this is not a selfish love in which the Christian community fails to face out to the world. Christians are to abound in love to "all men." They are to seek the good of all men. They are to find an example of Christian love in the compassion toward them and all men that they have seen in the lives of Paul,

Silas, and Timothy. And they are to realize that these men have caught something of the compassion of Jesus.

The prayer for the Thessalonians is made in order that the Lord may establish their hearts "unblamable in holiness before our God and Father, at the coming of our Lord Jesus with all his saints" (vs. 13). Growth in love is essential if Christians are to be ready to meet the Lord at his coming. When Paul speaks of the coming of the Lord Jesus "with all his saints," he is probably thinking of the hope that when Jesus comes he will bring with him those who have fallen asleep in him. But the word which is translated "saints" could refer also to angels. Although here, as elsewhere, Paul is thinking definitely of the return of Christ, his idea applies with equal force to the meeting of the believer with Christ at death. In either case it is clear that while we may fail in other things, we must not fail in Christian love. Paul does not deal here with the springs of Christian love, but he does insist on the supreme place of love in the Christian life. This idea is elaborated in the familiar thirteenth chapter of First Corinthians.

FOR THE STRENGTHENING OF THE CHURCH

I Thessalonians 4:1—5:28

The Plea for Purity (4:1-8)

The movement of the letter has been brought to a suitable stopping point. An appropriate closing prayer has been made. Then Paul adds two more chapters.

Timothy had just come to Paul from Thessalonica. Paul had talked intimately with him concerning the spiritual condition of the church. On the whole Timothy's report was most encouraging. But there were places at which the life of the congregation needed to be strengthened. So, instead of closing his letter, Paul adds a series of postscripts in which he deals with matters of special interest.

It is interesting to observe that the first of these is the call to purity. The church at Thessalonica was made up of Jews and Gentiles. The Jews were in danger of turning the doctrine of Christian liberty into license. And the Gentile Christians in their pagan religions had not known a faith that curbed the passions of men. It was difficult to feel a sense of guilt in the presence of the gods of Greece and Rome. Paul had to make it absolutely clear that the Christian life involved purity in sexual relations.

He approaches this difficult subject with his usual tact. He reminds his readers of the instructions on the meaning of Christian purity which he had given to them when he was with them. As in his dealing with Christian love, he is careful to pay tribute to the remarkable progress toward purity which had already been made. The church at Thessalonica stood out as a center of purity in the midst of the lax sexual relations of the Grecian world. Paul, moreover, does not mention any specific cases of impurity. His words are merely intended to strengthen and enforce the will to purity which was already present in the church.

The instructions which Paul had given the Thessalonians when he was with them were "through the Lord Jesus" (4:2). Jesus had repudiated the Mosaic permission of divorce and had set for the Christian community the ideal of marriage as a lifelong commitment between one man and one woman (Matt. 19:3-9). He had insisted on purity of inner thought and life (Matt. 5:27-32). The Christian ideal of marriage is rooted in the words of the Lord.

Against the background of the teaching of the Lord, Paul tells the Thessalonians that the will of God for them is their sanctification. This basic truth could be applied in various areas of moral endeavor. But Paul does not want them to miss his specific meaning: the will of God for them is that they abstain from sexual immorality. While the central meaning is crystal-clear, there is some uncertainty about the proper translation of verses 4 and 5. Many interpreters feel that Paul divides his advice into two parts. In the first he urges everyone who is married to strive to appreciate his own partner. Regardless of whether or not this is the actual meaning of Paul's language, it is good advice. One way to purity is for those who live within the marriage relation to seek constantly to appreciate each other. Turning his attention to those who are facing marriage, Paul insists that every person should seek a life partner in holiness and honor, not in the passion of lust like the heathen who know not God. True Christian marriage is to be approached in holiness and in honor, with full acceptance of its responsibilities and with no intention of using another person for the selfish satisfaction of lust.

Paul's teaching had been "that no man transgress, and wrong his brother in this matter, because the Lord is an avenger in all these things" (vs. 6). This affirms that all sins of sex involve a wrong to persons. The wrong may be to the woman whose purity is violated. It may also be to her husband or her parents. And in many cases the deepest wrong may be to a life born out of wedlock. God is concerned about the sins of impurity because they always involve wrongs to persons. And the Thessalonians are reminded that the Lord is an avenger in these things. God has so ordered his moral universe that those who violate the Christian ideal of purity are certain to reap the consequences of their evildoing. Verse 7 reiterates the fact that God has not called us for uncleanness, but in holiness.

In verse 8, attention is called to God's gift of his Holy Spirit. Christians must walk by the Spirit and not by the lust of the flesh. The man who disregards the inner promptings of the Spirit disregards not man, but God. When a man yields to the sins of impurity, he is violating the will of the God who has given him his sanctifying Spirit. It is clear that in the divine intention the Christian community is to be a community of purity in which believers respond to the God who has called them to holiness. There was to be no mistaking of Paul's meaning at this point.

Concerning Love and Labor (4:9-12)

Paul returns to a theme which always deeply concerns him. Although he has discussed Christian love in 3:11-13, he must emphasize again his deep concern that the Christian community should be a brotherhood in which the various members are bound to one another in Christian love. The Thessalonians have been "taught by God to love one another." We think here of the familiar words of First John: "In this is love, not that we loved God but that he loved us and sent his Son to be the expiation for our sins. Beloved, if God so loved us, we also ought to love one another" (I John 4:10-11). The springs of Christian love are found in responding to the Son of God who loved us and gave himself for us (Gal. 2:20). We love because Christ first loved us (I John 4:19). The cutting edge of the Christian community in its impact on the secular world of the first century was the power by which men were lifted out of their isolation and set in the midst of a community of love.

Verse 11 passes from the exhortation to love to the command to work. There is a close connection between the two ideas. The Christian fellowship as a community of love assumed some responsibility for the welfare of all of its members. While there is

here no common ownership of goods, the hungry were fed, the
naked were clothed, and the sick were nursed. But a community
of love which seeks to see that the basic needs of all of its members are cared for will soon disintegrate unless it becomes also a
community of labor. This is true of large family units in our society today. The family group cannot look after the needs of its
members unless each able-bodied member takes his full share of
the labor involved. The Thessalonians therefore are to be ready
to work with their hands as Paul has instructed them. The no-
bility and the dignity of manual labor are here recognized. Paul
himself was not ashamed to earn his living by weaving tents. Two
reasons for work are set forth. The first is that the Christians
"may command the respect of outsiders." The Christians are to
be known as industrious. In the second place, each Christian is
to seek to support himself and in this way to maintain his independence. It is clear from this that the Christian fellowship was
to minister only to those who for one reason or another were
unable to earn a living themselves. In II Thessalonians 3:6-13
Paul gives more extended treatment to the necessity for Christian labor.

Concerning Those Who Are Asleep (4:13-18)

The passage in which the Christian hope concerning those
who have fallen asleep in Christ is set forth is the most important
single passage in the Letters to the Thessalonians. Some of the
language of this passage has been incorporated into almost every
funeral service. The passage concerns us as much as it did the
Thessalonians, since it deals with the hope of life after death. It
is important therefore to look at the passage in its original setting. Timothy had doubtless told Paul of deaths which had taken
place in the Christian community at Thessalonica. The friends of
those who were dead experienced the natural concern of all men
for the state of the dead. In particular, they were concerned as
to whether or not those who had died would share in the salvation which Christ was to bring at his return. It should be remembered that both Paul and the Thessalonians expected the return
of Christ in the near future. The fifth chapter deals with the elements of uncertainty in this expectation (see comment). It is
sufficient here to realize that the concern of the Thessalonians
was expressed against the background of the expectation of the
return of Christ in a comparatively short time.

Paul tells the Thessalonians that although it is not improper to feel grief at the death of a loved one, Christians should not sorrow as those who have no hope. The basis of the Christian hope is then set forth: "We believe that Jesus died and rose again" (vs. 14). This belief, held in common by Paul and the Thessalonian Christians, is the great conviction that is central to the proclamation of the gospel of Jesus Christ. The foundations of this conviction are not given here; they are to be found in I Corinthians 15:3-11, where the witness of the Apostles and the early Christian community and Paul's own vision of the Risen Lord are included in the testimony.

The resurrection of Jesus Christ was central to the thinking of Paul and the New Testament Christians as they confronted death. They believed that God had brought again from the dead the Lord Jesus Christ through the blood of the everlasting Covenant (Heb. 13:20). They knew that Jesus had manifested himself as alive to his disciples "by many proofs," appearing to them during forty days and speaking to them of the Kingdom of God (Acts 1:3). They were confident that the resurrection of Jesus was a revelation of the reality of the resurrection world which lies beyond death. They believed that Jesus was living in this invisible world of spiritual reality. They believed that in time there would be a full disclosure of the world to which the Risen Lord bore witness. Because his thinking starts with the fact of the Resurrection, Paul can write: "Since we believe that Jesus died and rose again, even so, through Jesus, God will bring with him those who have fallen asleep." The connection between the two parts of this statement is not obvious. It is one thing to believe that Jesus died and rose again; it is quite another to believe that God will bring with Jesus at his coming those who have fallen asleep in him. Paul supports his statement by citing an unrecorded word of the Lord that the living and the dead will participate alike in the salvation which Christ is to bring. It is needless to speculate as to where Paul received this word of the Lord. He may preserve for us here a word of the Risen Lord spoken to his disciples concerning the Kingdom of God, or he may be giving a direct revelation which had been given to him. In either case, he is confident that he speaks the word of the Lord when he says that the living and the dead will share alike in Christ's salvation. The phrase, "the word of the Lord," applies to verse 15, not to the description of the return of the Lord.

In I Thessalonians 4:16-17 the imagery of Jewish apocalypse is used to set forth in vivid fashion the Christian hope of the Lord's return. We see the Lord descending from heaven. We hear his cry of command. We hear also the archangel's call and the sound of the trumpet of God. We face the resurrection morning in which the dead in Christ rise first. We are given a vivid picture of the way in which living believers are caught up together with them in the air. The picture closes as the living and the dead are united to be forever with one another and with the Lord.

Did Paul intend this picture to be taken literally? We know of course that he shared the world view of his time. He believed in a three-storied universe, with heaven above, earth beneath, and Hades below. It was natural therefore for him to think of Jesus as coming from heaven and of the saints as caught up together with him into heaven. Our view of the universe is not the same as Paul's. We know that beyond the earth there are infinite reaches of space. The picture which Paul painted could have little meaning for modern man if taken literally. But Paul was not so naïve as to believe that the event which he sets forth here could take place without a radical transformation of the whole nature of our universe. There is a similar picture at the close of the third chapter of Philippians, where Paul writes: "But our commonwealth is in heaven, and from it we await a Savior, the Lord Jesus Christ, who will change our lowly body to be like his glorious body, by the power which enables him even to subject all things to himself" (Phil. 3:20-21). Here "heaven" is identical with the world of the resurrection, and our entrance into it is conditioned upon Christ's power to work in us a radical change in which the body of our humiliation is transformed into the likeness of his own glorious body. A similar transformation is posited in the discussion of the resurrection hope in I Corinthians 15:42-54.

Paul starts with the resurrection of Christ. He moves from his belief in the reality of the resurrection body of the Lord to the assurance of the world of heaven, to the belief in a world of spiritual reality which is at present invisible to man. This is the world of which we usually think when we speak of heaven. And Paul is confident that the world we know will finally be consummated in the full disclosure of the resurrection world. At present it is possible to speak of the world of heaven only in symbolism.

When we understand this we can realize that the symbolism which Paul employs is as effective as any we could invent today. We miss Paul's meaning when we insist on a literal interpretation of language which was never intended to be understood in this way.

When Paul wrote I Thessalonians 4:13-18, the expectancy of the immediate return of the Lord dominated his thought, but he had already laid hold of the idea of the union of the believer and Christ which takes place at death. The clear meaning of 5:10 is that believers who have died are living with Jesus. In Philippians, where Paul faces the possibility of death in the near future, he writes, "For to me to live is Christ, and to die is gain," and interprets death in terms of departing and being with Christ (Phil. 1:21, 23). In II Corinthians 5:8, Paul understands that death for the Christian involves being away from the earthly body and being at home with the Lord. On the basis of these statements, it is fair to say that Paul believed that those who died in the Lord survived the crisis of physical death and entered a world in which they were alive with Christ. He believed also in an ultimate consummation of history which involved the full disclosure of the world of God, with a fundamental change in the structure of our universe and a radical transformation of the nature of man to fit him for life in this new environment. He was confident of the reunion of believers in a world in which they would be together with one another and with the Lord. This hope was rooted in his belief that Jesus died and rose again, and on this basis he urged the Thessalonian Christians to comfort one another concerning those who were asleep.

Concerning the Times and the Seasons (5:1-11)

It is appropriate that the vivid picture of the return of the Lord should be followed by some admonitions concerning the times and the seasons. Christians should not find in the hope of the Lord's return an excuse for idleness. The Christians at Thessalonica knew that the day of the Lord would come as "a thief in the night." The illustration is selected to show the uncertainty of the exact time of the coming of the Lord. Paul must have been familiar with the tradition preserved in Acts in which the risen Lord tells his disciples that it is not for them "to know times or seasons which the Father has fixed by his own authority" (Acts 1:7). The Lord had told the disciples to con-

centrate on the giving of their witness to him and to leave
to the Father in heaven the disclosure of the times and the seasons. Paul also uses the illustration of the coming of travail upon
a woman with child (5:3). In the coming of the thief and the
coming of travail, the emphasis is on the suddenness of the
coming. When the hour has come it will be too late to begin
to get ready for it. Christians must live so as to be ready at any
time to give an account of themselves to their Lord.

In the verses which follow, Paul spells out the meaning of
this watchful waiting for the coming of the Lord. Christians are
children of the light, "sons of the day." They are to be found
awake and sober. There follows a description of the Christian
soldier. First Thessalonians 5:8 should be compared with the
more detailed description of the Christian soldier in Ephesians
6:13-17. In either case, there is a picture of one who is alert
and ready for the time of testing.

The thought of the "hope of salvation" leads Paul to write:
"God has not destined us for wrath, but to obtain salvation
through our Lord Jesus Christ, who died for us so that whether
we wake or sleep we might live with him." The Thessalonians
felt that they had been called of God into the fellowship of his
church; they were confident that God had destined them, not for
wrath, but for salvation through Jesus Christ. The wrath which
is referred to here is the wrath of God on sinful men, from
which Jesus has delivered those who are his. Because of this
they can face with confidence a disclosure of God which would
otherwise be a time of judgment and condemnation. Because of
their knowledge of God's purpose of salvation in Jesus Christ,
Christians are to "encourage one another and build one another
up." And for a further word of encouragement, Paul reminds
the Thessalonians that this is what they are now doing.

The Government of the Church (5:12-13)

There is no conscious attempt in these verses to set forth the
government of the church, but close scrutiny will yield some
fruitful suggestions. There were obviously, among the Thessalonians, some who labored "among" them and were "over" them
in the Lord. Upon these men there rested the responsibility of
admonishing the other members of the church. They were to
be esteemed highly in the Lord because of their work. The ad-
monition, "Be at peace among yourselves," may have no rela-

tion to the discipline of the church. But its insertion at this point would suggest that the peace of the church is to be found in respect and love for the duly constituted officers of the church. Acts 14:23 indicates that on the first missionary journey, Paul and Barnabas appointed elders in every church. It would be reasonable to think that Paul had appointed elders for the church at Thessalonica. In the Letter to the Philippians, bishops and deacons are mentioned in the greeting (Phil. 1:1). This letter was written to the church that Paul established immediately before he came to Thessalonica. We may surmise therefore that he had also appointed deacons in the church at Thessalonica. Many of the problems of discipline of the church at Thessalonica seem to have centered in the administration of relief. In Acts, the "seven," who are often thought of as deacons, had been appointed to prevent the Apostles from becoming absorbed in the serving of tables (Acts 6:1-6). Very little is known about the government of the church at Thessalonica. But when I Thessalonians 5:12-14 is combined with II Thessalonians 3:6-13 it becomes plain that this was a community which had an accepted leadership and a pattern for enforcing conformity to the standards of the Christian community. Here are the beginnings of the concern for church government which finds fuller expression in the Pastoral Epistles.

The Worthy Life (5:14-22)

As this letter is brought to a close, a number of practical injunctions are given. These various exhortations do not seem to be closely connected. They must be seen, however, in the light of the message of the letter as a whole. In 2:12 the readers were charged to "lead a life worthy of God," who calls them into his own Kingdom and glory. But it is necessary now for Paul to be specific and to state the Christian ideal of conduct in terms that all can understand. The Christians are to "admonish the idle, encourage the fainthearted, help the weak, be patient with them all." A full statement of the Christian ideal of returning good for evil is also set forth: "See that none of you repays evil for evil, but always seek to do good to one another and to all." The Christian community, moreover, was to be marked by its joyousness, its constant dependence on God in prayer, and its readiness to give thanks for all things. These marks of Christian character were to be understood as representing the will of God in Christ. They were to face the various experiences of life as part of the discipline of God for them.

The readers are urged to remain sensitive to the movings of the Spirit (vs. 19). They must not throw cold water on ideas that may be the promptings of the Spirit. The living Church must wait for the guidance of the Holy Spirit. A study of I Corinthians 14:20-33 provides a description of early Christian worship as a setting in which Paul's injunctions are appropriate. The Church must remain sensitive to the will of God as expressed in the promptings of the Spirit or in prophesying, but the Christians are not to accept as the will of God every half-baked idea which comes to them. They are to test everything and to hold fast only to what is good. Verse 22 can be translated, "abstain from every form of evil" or "abstain from every appearance of evil," but the first is probably the better translation. Evil can arise in many forms. Its approaches must be recognized and its evil suggestions refused. It is also true that things which have the appearance of evil should be shunned.

The Faithfulness of God (5:23-28)

Paul is now ready to finish his letter, and again he expresses himself in a prayer for his converts, this one addressed to "the God of peace." He refers to God in this way in three other places (Rom. 15:33; 16:20; and Phil. 4:9; see also Hebrews 13:20, in which the writer of Hebrews begins his great benediction by addressing God as "the God of peace"). In I Corinthians 14:33, Paul writes: ". . . God is not a God of confusion but of peace." God calls all men to accept his offer of salvation and be at peace with him. Peace between man and man also comes when those who are at peace with God walk in a manner which is worthy of their high calling. The prayer for the Thessalonians is that the God of peace will sanctify them wholly. This idea is elaborated in the petition, "may your spirit and soul and body be kept sound and blameless at the coming of our Lord Jesus Christ." Paul's prayer is that the process of growth in holiness which has already started in his converts may be continued until they have become Christlike in character. There need not be much concern over an apparent division of the human personality into "spirit and soul and body." Paul was not giving a course in psychology. The redemption which Christ brings involves the whole person: this is the core of the Christian hope of the resurrection of the body. While the Greeks depreciated the body and looked forward to the immortality of the soul apart from the body, the Christians looked for a redemption in which both soul and body were preserved. The prayer of Paul which refers specifically to the preservation of his converts in the hour of judgment at Jesus' return can apply also to God's power to keep us in the hour of death.

"He who calls you is faithful, and he will do it" (5:24). This is the central theme of the Bible: the faithfulness of God in spite of the faithlessness of his people. The God who has begun his work of redemption in the hearts of the Thessalonian converts will continue to work with them until he has perfected them in holiness and has brought them into his eternal Kingdom. This is not to deny the element of human response or to cut the nerve of man's responsibility. But it does put the emphasis on God's faithfulness in bringing to completion the work he has started.

In the closing verses of the epistle Paul refers to his converts three times as "brethren." He asks them to pray for him and he sends greetings to all of them. The forcefulness of the language in verse 27 may suggest that some of the brethren did not wish to hear this letter. Here we have the beginning of that process in which the letters of Paul were read aloud in the churches. It was in this way that these letters came in time to be accepted in all the churches and to take their place in that body of writings which was to become the New Testament. The last two verses of Second Thessalonians indicate that Paul was accustomed to write the last line of a letter in his own hand as a mark of identification to prevent the circulation of letters forged in his name. A glance at II Thessalonians 2:2 shows that there was need for such caution. Paul surely closed the present letter in his own handwriting and with the characteristic phrase, "The grace of our Lord Jesus Christ be with you."

DELIVERANCE AND JUDGMENT

II Thessalonians 1:1-12

Steadfastness in Persecution (1:1-4)

The Second Letter to the Thessalonians must have been written some months after the first. Probably Paul wrote this letter after he had received from his messenger some account of the reactions of the Thessalonians to the earlier one. The greetings in the second letter are similar to those in the first. In both, Silas and Timothy are listed with Paul as writers. In the first letter Paul refers to God as *the* Father and in the second as *our* Father. The emphasis in the first may be on God's relation to Jesus; in the second letter it is on his relation to us. It is remarkable that only two decades after the death of Christ he is associated with God the Father as the source of grace and peace (vs. 2).

The thanksgiving of the Apostle for the brethren at Thessalonica is based on the fact that their faith is growing abundantly and that their love for each other is increasing (vs. 3; compare I Thess. 3:12; 4:9-11). In referring to their growth in faith, he may be thinking of the way in which the faith of his converts has stood the test of persecution. In the former letter he commented on the reports of the faith of the Thessalonians which had come to him (I Thess. 1:9). In the second letter he says that he and Timothy and Silas are boasting of the Thessalonians in the churches of God. This boasting is based on the steadfastness and faith which the Thessalonians are showing in persecutions and afflictions.

The reference to persecution is the key to the passage which follows. The first letter indicates that the Thessalonians suffered persecutions from their own countrymen just as the churches in Judea had faced persecutions from the Jews. Paul had sent Timothy back to Thessalonica to strengthen the hearts of his converts in such a time of persecution. Aparently the opposition of the pagan community to the church at Thessalonica had been intensified in the period between the letters. This is shown by the way in which the Thessalonians hope for deliverance from their afflictions and in their concern that those who are persecuting them shall not escape the righteous judgment of God. Men do not cry out for deliverance until persecution has become intense.

The Hope of a Deliverance (1:5-7)

In writing to the persecuted church, Paul pictures the coming of the Lord as the day of deliverance. Whereas in First Thessalonians the purpose was to assure the Christians that those who die in the Lord will share the glories of the Messianic salvation with those who are alive when Christ returns, II Thessalonians 1:5-12 was written to assure the persecuted Christians at Thessalonica that the coming of the Lord would be for them a time of deliverance and for their persecutors a time of judgment. While Paul consistently refused to assign a date for the coming of the Lord, he expected the return of Christ in the comparatively near future. At various times in the history of the Christian Church, Christians in the midst of persecutions and afflictions have looked to the return of Christ as a day of deliverance for them and as a time of judgment on those who reject the gospel.

The fidelity of the Thessalonian Christians in the midst of their persecutions was a sign that God had indeed deemed them worthy of the Kingdom. The language of verse 5 also suggests that the afflictions which they were facing might be part of the discipline through which God was preparing them for their heavenly home. They were suffering because of their loyalty to Jesus; certainly it must be part of the righteous government of God in the ordering of his universe to grant them rest when their suffering had accomplished his purpose in them, and also to bring to judgment those who had so brutally oppressed them.

The Judgment of the Wicked (1:8-9)

In the first letter Paul had told his converts never to repay evil with evil but always to seek to do good to one another and to all men (I Thess. 5:15). In such a way of life Christians were to imitate their Lord. The Apostle sees no contradiction between this summary of the way of life which Jesus taught and the thought of Jesus as judge (see also II Cor. 5:10). There is a difference between the wrath of the Lord who is the vindicator of the moral order of the universe and the conduct of individual Christians. In a similar situation Paul told the Romans never to avenge themselves, not to take in their hands the administering

of the judgments of God. They could refrain from revenge in
the confidence that God would not permit men to sin with im-
punity (Rom. 12:19).

The judgment which Jesus administers is visited "upon those
who do not know God and upon those who do not obey the
gospel of our Lord Jesus" (II Thess. 1:8). There is a great
dividing line between those who accept the gospel and those who
reject its message. Men are judged by the attitude which they
have taken to Jesus Christ and his offer of salvation.

Paul did not define the phrase "eternal destruction," but probably the core of its meaning for him was found in the succeed-
ing idea: "exclusion from the presence of the Lord." Hell involves eternal banishment and separation from the presence of
the Lord. Those who receive this judgment go out into a Christ-
less eternity. Their banishment means separation from God and
failure to realize the true destiny of man, which is to glorify
God and to enjoy him forever.

The Salvation of Believers (1:10-12)

The two verses just considered are the only verses in the Letters to the Thessalonians which indicate the fate of those who
reject the gospel. On the other hand, the letters are filled with
verses which set forth the Christian hope. Verses 10-12 pass at
once from the description of judgment to the positive picture
of the salvation of believers. Those who have believed will be
saved. Salvation comes to those who have believed the testimony
to Christ which has been delivered to them.

This section is closed with a prayer that God may make the
believers worthy of his call and that through his power he will
enable them to live in a manner that is worthy of their call.
God's call to them has been mediated through the preaching of
Paul. They have responded to it. But the call involves their
growth in holiness until they are fitted for their high calling.
The great purpose of God's work in them is that the name of
the Lord Jesus may be glorified in them. Jesus is glorified in his
saints as he perfects them in holiness and presents them blameless in the presence of his Father. And in the long reaches of
eternity he is glorified in them because of what he has done in
and through them, and they are glorified in him. They receive
glory through what he has done for them.

What is the meaning for Christians today in this picture of

the return of Christ as deliverer and judge? Paul and his converts held high expectation of the return of Christ in the not
too distant future. This expectation colors all of this letter. There
is some reference to it in every chapter. And Paul's ideas of
deliverance and judgment are therefore focused primarily upon
the return of Christ. In the perspective of history we know that
Paul and his converts were wrong in assuming that Jesus would
return in such a way as to bring an immediate and supernatural
deliverance to the persecuted Thessalonians. The Thessalonians
were not delivered by a spectacular return of Jesus with his
mighty angels in a flame of fire.

Are Paul's ideas concerning deliverance and judgment therefore to be permanently discredited? By no means. Christians
are still to look for a consummation of this present age in the return of Christ. And Christians still feel that the return of Christ
will be for his followers a time of vindication and for his enemies
a time of judgment. But when we speak of the return of Christ
we should realize that we are speaking of an event which cannot
be described in the categories of this present world. We are
thinking of an ultimate act of God, the full content of which
cannot be fully disclosed. When Paul sought to describe it he
was forced to employ the language of Jewish eschatology. He
would have been the first to admit that such language was inadequate. Similar language may be used today if we realize that
we are dealing in symbolism and not with language which is to
be taken with literal exactness.

While Christians today can look forward to the consummation of the age with the return of Christ, after a waiting period
of two thousand years they cannot live in the atmosphere of
immediate expectation which characterized the Early Church.
The eschatological tension of the New Testament, however, can
be recaptured if we think of the permanent tension between life
in this present world and life in the resurrection world which
Christ revealed. And we can feel the urgent necessity of being
ready at all times to meet our Lord, in the knowledge of the
crisis through which each individual must pass in the experience
of death and in the hope of entering heaven.

Against the background of this understanding of our human
situation today, Paul's ideas concerning deliverance and judgment can be disentangled from his expectation of the immediate
return of the Lord and be presented in a meaningful form. The

faithfulness of Christians in the midst of persecutions as a sign that they are deemed worthy of the Kingdom of God can have meaning for Christians who today are suffering for Christ's sake. The faith that the righteous judgment of God must in the end involve rest for believers and judgment for those who persecute them is valid for life today. In many cases it is not necessary to wait for life in another world to see this judgment. The saints who suffer for righteousness' sake receive their own deep satisfactions. And evil continues to carry in itself the seeds of its own destruction. Christians who suffer for their faith have a right to hope for vindication within this life and to expect that the events of history will in time force their persecutors to reap the consequences of their evil deeds. Suffering Christians, moreover, can be certain of their vindication in the life beyond the grave. Their persecutors will have to face the final judgment of Christ and receive from him good or evil according to what they have done in the body.

These verses also draw a great line of division between those who believe the message of the gospel and those who do not obey the gospel of our Lord Jesus Christ. This line of division is valid in our contemporary world. The utter seriousness of our life in this present world is that in it we may be called upon to make decisions which are eternal in their consequences. The passage closes with a picture of Christ as glorified in his people and of them as glorified in him, a picture which can properly be taken to describe the believer's hope of heaven today.

THE REVELATION OF THE MAN OF SIN

II Thessalonians 2:1-12

Paul's Purpose in This Passage (2:1-2)

Here begins one of the most difficult passages in Paul's Letters to the Thessalonians. Because of the intense interest in any passage of Scripture which can be interpreted as predicting the future, this passage has received attention out of proportion to its real significance. It is important first of all to try to understand what Paul meant to say to his Thessalonian converts when he wrote it, and then some questions may be raised concerning its significance for Christians today.

Paul had already dealt with "the times and the seasons" (I

Thess. 5:1-11). In the first letter he had insisted that the time of
the return of the Lord was not definitely known. Its coming, like
the coming of the thief in the night, is apt to occur when it is least
expected. When Paul wrote Second Thessalonians he had apparently received from Thessalonica some reports which disturbed
him. It would seem that some of his converts had become so certain
of the coming of Christ in the immediate future that they saw
no need for work. They must have felt that there was no reason to save for a distant future since the coming of the Lord
was now a question of days. It would seem also that those who
held this view appealed to the words of Paul, and possibly to a
letter which they claimed was from him, to support their position.

It is clear that Paul, at this stage in his development, did
show an absorbing interest in the return of Christ. The references to the Second Coming in First Thessalonians could easily
have been interpreted to mean that the coming was imminent.
Paul's central purpose, therefore, in writing Second Thessalonians was to correct a distortion of his views of the Second
Coming. He did not want his disciples thinking that the return
of Christ was so near that there was no necessity for work. He
may have been concerned lest an overemphasis on the second
coming of Christ cut the nerve of missionary endeavor. Even
today we are apt to find that when people become absorbed in
talking about the end of the world they tend to lose interest in
plans to improve life in this world and in long-range plans for
the establishment of the Church in all nations.

Paul's purpose therefore was very practical. He wished to make
it clear that the coming of the Lord was not immediately at
hand. There are some things which must happen before the Lord
returns.

The Expectation of Antichrist (2:3-4)

It should be remembered that Paul could assume on the part
of his readers a knowledge of some teachings concerning the
order of events leading up to the return of Christ with which
he and they were familiar (see vs. 5). We do not have these
teachings, and therefore many references which would be understood by the Thessalonians are not clear to us. It would seem
that there was in the Christian community at this time the expectation of the appearance of a man who would become the
embodiment of the opposition of the pagan world to the gospel.

At a later date we find in the Letters of John the expectation of the coming of "antichrist." John's letters were written to combat the idea that the first coming of Christ was not a true incarnation of God in the flesh but merely the appearance of a god who seemed to be man. John defined the spirit of "antichrist" as a denial that Jesus Christ had come in the flesh (see I John 2:18, 22; 4:3; II John 7).

Paul does not use the word "antichrist," but he does write of the appearance of one whom he calls a "man of sin" or a "man of lawlessness." Before the coming of the Lord there will be a "rebellion" or a "falling away." We do not know what he means here, but he probably does not refer to the falling away of Christians, for he expected the Thessalonians to be saved. There is a vivid description of "the man of lawlessness." He is one who opposes every so-called god or object of worship. He takes his seat in the temple of God. He proclaims himself to be God. He, therefore, will be a false Christ or a rival Christ.

The Restraining Power (2:5-7)

This man of sin has not yet appeared. He has not been made manifest because there is some power that is restraining him. We have no idea of the real nature of this restraining power. Some interpreters have felt that Paul referred to the Roman Empire, which at this time was protecting him. A few think that Paul's ministry to the Gentiles is the restraining power. Others think that the reference is to some supernatural power. Whatever the identification, Paul feels that the time for the revelation of the man of sin is not distant.

The Destruction of Antichrist (2:8)

In true apocalyptic fashion, Paul pictures the final unveiling of the man of sin, the signal for the return of Christ. Whereas in the first chapter the return of Christ is depicted as a time of deliverance for persecuted Christians and a time of judgment for their persecutors (1:7-10), here it is the time for the destruction of the power of the lawless one.

The Appeal of the Lawless One (2:9-12)

The conflict between Christ and the man of sin is not described in detail. Instead the activity of the lawless one in the period between his manifestation and the return of Christ is treated. He is to come as an expression of the activity of Satan. He is to come with power and with pretended signs and wonders. Here, as in the New Testament as a whole, miracles are not necessarily the signs of the working of God, for they may be expressions of the power of evil spirits. Our Lord's miracles are significant not only because of their power but also because of their moral quality.

The appeal of the man of sin will be to those who have rejected the gospel. He will appeal to those who did not believe the truth but had pleasure in unrighteousness. Paul writes as a Jew. He often overlooks second causes and attributes everything that happens directly to the activity of God. But the principle which he expresses is sound. When men harden their hearts against the acceptance of the gospel they prepare the way to embrace some "strong delusion." Men in our own time have rejected the gospel and then have believed that their salvation was to be found through a police state or through the dictatorship of the working class. Similarly, when men reject the gospel in the name of science they are left with some idolatry which will in the end destroy them.

What value has this message of Paul for Christians today? We must state quite frankly that Paul was wrong in his immediate expectation. The man of sin whom he describes did not appear in any figure known to us in history. This is not to deny that some aspects of the character of this man of sin have been found in certain characters of history. But it is best to affirm that Paul, in his effort to convince the Thessalonians that the coming of Christ was not immediately at hand, made use of some apocalyptic teachings current in the first century that have not been fulfilled. And if we cannot identify Paul's man of sin with any of the figures of his century, it is absurd to think that we have here a blueprint of events which are yet to be realized. Paul was thinking of the first century, not the twentieth. Christians today can look forward to an ultimate consummation of the age in the return of Christ. But they will not find an outline for the events of the future in "the little apocalypse" which Paul gave to the Thessalonians.

But this does not mean that Paul's message is without value to Christians today. We can share with him his practical purpose of turning the attention of his converts away from speculative questions about the time of Christ's return and setting them to work at the tasks before them. All too often the concentration of Christians on the fulfillment of prophecy has been associated with withdrawal from the actual tasks of the Kingdom of God in the world. And we are true to the spirit of Paul in this passage when we think of the conflict between Christ and the powers of evil as growing in intensity as the gospel wins its way in the hearts of men. We are true also to the thought of Paul when we think of the forces of evil as deifying themselves and presenting themselves as ways of salvation for mankind. Some of the great conflicts of our time are between Christ and secular forces which offer themselves as religions. And Christians today can share with Paul his confidence that Jesus Christ is the Lord of history. While no one individual can be identified as antichrist, it is certain that the spirit of antichrist has appeared at various times in history and that it will continue to appear in the various idolatries that claim the loyalties of men. But God's people can be confident that the ultimate decisions of history are in the hands of the One whom Christians acknowledge as Lord and Savior. Greater is he that is for us than he that is against us.

CONCLUDING REMARKS

II Thessalonians 2:13—3:18

The Calling of the Saints (2:13-15)

In his description of the followers of the man of sin, Paul traced the process of hardening which comes to those who reject the gospel. The way of evil leads men to increasing blindness, in which they give themselves to some delusion which is certain in the end to destroy them. Over against this dark picture the destiny of those who accept Jesus as Lord and Savior is painted in bright colors. These verses are a summary of the plan of redemption. The salvation of the believers is traced back to a divine election, in which God chose them to be saved. Here as always election includes selection for service. The church at Thessalonica is God's instrument for the redemption of its community even as Paul is called to be the Apostle to the Gentiles.

The call of God had come to the Thessalonians through the proclamation of the gospel there by Paul, Silas, and Timothy. It had become effective in the lives of the Thessalonian Christians through their belief in the truth and through sanctification by the Spirit. The two sides of the process are not to be separated. It was through the witness of the Spirit in their hearts that the members of the church at Thessalonica had accepted Paul's message as the word of God and had acknowledged Jesus Christ as Lord (see I Thess. 1:5; 2:13; I Cor. 12:3). But after the Thessalonian Christians had entered upon the life of faith through belief in the truth of the gospel, it had been the special work of the Holy Spirit to enable them to grow in holiness.

Here, then, is a great summary: The call which comes from God is an expression of the redemptive purpose that has been in the heart of God from the beginning. The redemption is made possible through the death of Christ for us. The knowledge of the gospel comes to the Thessalonians in the preaching of Paul. It becomes effective for salvation through the faith of the Thessalonians and through the work of the Holy Spirit in their hearts. Its ultimate purpose is that these believers may lay hold of the glory of the Lord Jesus.

The reference to the glory of Jesus Christ does not blind the Apostle to the realities of the present. He knows that his converts are being tested in the furnace of persecution. Therefore he urges them to stand firm and to hold to "the traditions" which they have received from him. It is interesting to observe that we have in this letter, which is among the first of the letters of Paul, reference to a tradition which is already recognized as essential to the Christian faith. The content of this tradition is not defined here. It must have included, however, a narrative of the major events in the life of Jesus and a record of some of his sayings. It would have included also an interpretation of the significance of events such as the death and resurrection of Jesus as they were understood in the Early Church. (When the word "tradition" is used in 3:6 it clearly refers to specific instructions which Paul has given concerning the necessity of work on the part of all the members of the church.) There are various places in the letters of Paul in which he summarizes essential elements in the Christian tradition, for example, Romans 10:8-13; I Corinthians 15: 3-11; and Galatians 1:6-17. This reference to the Christian tradition in an early letter from Paul prepares us for the strong emphasis on "the deposit of faith" which is found in the Letters to Timothy. The tradition was in part oral, and Paul had certainly taught it by word of mouth. But it was already in process of being written down. Paul included elements of it in his Letters to the Thessalonians. Now he urges the Thessalonians to hold firmly to these traditions which they have been taught. Their fidelity in this respect is an indication of the genuineness of their conversion and the certainty of their obtaining the glory of the Lord Jesus Christ.

A Prayer for the Thessalonians (2:16—3:5)

Paul brings his letter to a close with a prayer for his Thessalonian converts (2:16-17). Then he asks them to pray for him (3:1-2). He breaks the movement of his thought with two verses in which he affirms the faithfulness of the Lord and his confidence in the obedience of the Thessalonians (3:3-4). He then brings the paragraph to a close with a final prayer for his converts (3:5).

The prayer is directed to "our Lord Jesus Christ himself, and God our Father." Once again the Lord Jesus Christ and God the Father are set side by side as those to whom Christians should pray. There is a glance back to what has already happened—God the Father and the Lord Jesus Christ "loved us and gave us eternal comfort and good hope through grace." God's gift has come not on the basis of our merit but through his infinite grace. With an assurance which is based on what God has already done, Paul prays that God will comfort the hearts of the Thessalonians and establish them in every good word and work. To "comfort" here means to encourage and to strengthen.

When the Apostle requests that the brethren pray for him, he suggests that they pray for two things. The first is for the blessing of God on the proclamation of the Word, probably the ministry in which Paul is now engaged in Corinth. There is here a dynamic concept of the word of the Lord which will speed on and triumph (3:1).

The second request is that the Thessalonians pray that Paul and Timothy and Silas "may be delivered from wicked and evil men." The comment is added: "for not all have faith." Here is a glimpse of the dangers which confronted Paul and his companions as they sought to give a faithful witness to the gospel in the city of Corinth. We know that later in his ministry there, the Jews in Corinth "made a united attack upon Paul and brought him before the tribunal" (Acts 18:12) for trial before Gallio, the proconsul. In this case, Paul was saved by the refusal of Gallio to pay any attention to the charges of the Jews.

But Paul's concern for his own safety does not occupy his attention very long. His mind goes back at once to his main concern—his desire to see the Thessalonians remain faithful in the midst of their afflictions. He deals with this concern in two ways. The first is an affirmation of the power of the Lord to keep those who are his in the day of testing (3:3). The second is an expression of confidence in the Thessalonians, that they are doing and will do the things which Paul commands (3:4). Again there is the language of prayer as the Apostle prays that the Lord will direct the hearts of his followers to the love of God. And then with a logical inconsistency, in which the same person is both subject and object in one sentence, he prays that the Lord will direct the hearts of his people to the steadfastness of Christ.

Concerning Idleness (3:6-13)

We can imagine that Paul in dictating his letter felt that he had brought it to a proper conclusion with the prayer we have just considered. But then he decided that he might not have been sufficiently clear in dealing with the persistent problem of idleness in the church. He takes therefore a fresh start in his attack on this problem. The natural tendency of all men to get out of work if they can was accentuated in Thessalonica by a distortion of Paul's emphasis on the return of Christ in the near future. In this passage, he adds to what he has already said (in I Thess. 4:11-12) the suggestion that discipline be enforced by a policy of separation from those living in idleness. This is group disapproval in order to bring about conformity to the accepted pattern of the group (see also 3:14-15). The command to work is supported by reference to Paul's own example while he was with them. Here again he was concerned to protect the right of those who preached the gospel. In administering the discipline of this church, Paul had given the command: "If any one will not work, let him not eat." In its original setting this oft-quoted sentence is simply a statement of a policy of sound administration of church benevolences. The members of the Thessalonian church who were able to work were not to be permitted to live off of the common funds of the church, unless they by their own labor were contributing to the resources of the Christian community. Such a principle is absolutely essential if genuine community life is to be maintained. And the command of Paul states in its simplest terms one of the major reasons for work. We must work if we would eat. We must work to provide the necessities of our human existence. The problem which Paul faced in Thessalonica is dealt with again in First Timothy 5:3-16.

The Beginnings of Church Discipline (3:14-15)

The use of group pressure is extended to the enforcement of obedience to what has been said in this letter and by implication to the whole matter of fidelity to the Christian tradition. Those who had identified themselves with the Christian communion at Thessalonica had done so at the cost of breaking with many of the associations which they had had in the Gentile world. In such a situation, approval or disapproval of the group with which he was now identified was a matter of great importance to each individual Christian. Paul was not dealing here with excommunication, in which a person is cast out of a fellowship. The offending members were not to be considered enemies; they were to be looked upon as brothers. But they were to be made to feel strongly the weight of group disapproval when they failed to conform to the accepted pattern. The purpose of this group disapproval was to bring the disobedient members back into line with the purposes of the group. There is nothing either Christian or unchristian about this kind of use of group pressure. It is practiced in one form or another by many groups today. But it is interesting to notice that this use of group pressure represented the beginning of Christian discipline. The method by which Paul expected group pressure to be exerted is not indicated. It could have been by action of the recognized leaders of the church. More probably it was a sort of voluntary group pressure exercised by the church members without any formal action by the church. In the latter pattern a similar form of group pressure is applied to their members by Christian churches today. The fear of losing group acceptance can still furnish powerful motivation for conformity to Christian standards of thought and action.

Benediction and Identification (3:16-18)

Having expressed himself on the discipline of the idlers, Paul is again ready to bring his letter to a close. He does so with a prayer to "the Lord of peace" which may have been suggested by his comments on the need of discipline for those who would not work. In any event, it is a prayer that Jesus will give peace to his followers at all times and in all ways.

Paul dictated his letters, perhaps because of trouble with his eyes. But at this point he took the pen and wrote: "I, Paul, write this greeting with my own hand. This is the mark in every letter of mine; it is the way I write. The grace of our Lord Jesus Christ be with you all" (3:17-18). In 2:2 he urged the Thessalonians not to be quickly shaken by a "letter purporting to be from us." Paul's opponents may have attempted to support their positions by circulating letters which they said were from Paul. These last lines are therefore identification and signature. We can imagine the way the leaders of the church examined the close of the letter when it was delivered. They knew Paul's handwriting and they could be confident that this letter was indeed from **Paul.**

THE FIRST AND SECOND LETTERS OF PAUL TO

TIMOTHY

THE LETTER OF PAUL TO

TITUS

INTRODUCTION

Letters to Pastors

The two Letters to Timothy and the Letter to Titus have long
been called "the Pastoral Epistles." The Letters to the Thessalonians are written to a church; these letters are addressed to individuals. However, they are not purely personal letters. They
are written to Timothy and Titus to guide them in their work as
pastors. While these letters deal at times with theology and contain some great doctrinal statements, in the main they are practical in their point of view, concerned with the qualifications of
church officers, with the capacity to distinguish between true and
false teaching, and with the preservation of the purity of the message of the gospel. They deal with such administrative details of
the work of pastors as the treatment of widows, the adaptation
of the message of the gospel to different age groups and to various class groups, and the conduct of public worship. These letters,
therefore, have always been helpful to any who are actively engaged in the work of the Church.

Date

In the New Testament, Second Thessalonians is followed by
First Timothy, but this does not mean that First Timothy was
written shortly after Second Thessalonians. First and Second
Thessalonians are probably the first of Paul's letters and can be
dated with reasonable accuracy about A.D. 50 or 51. Those who
feel that First and Second Timothy and Titus were written by
Paul are agreed that they are the last of his letters. Acceptance

of Pauline authorship does not guarantee complete accuracy in
dating, which depends on the whole reconstruction of the life of
Paul. But there is general agreement that the date of composi-
tion was about A.D. 65 to 67. Those who do not hold to the
Pauline authorship will vary even more greatly in their dating
of these letters, but most of them place them between the first
and the middle of the second century. In either case, we have
in the Letters to the Thessalonians and the Letters to Timothy
and Titus the contrast between the first and the last.

Authorship Affects Interpretation

Why is it that the Letters to the Thessalonians are universally
accepted as written by Paul, while there is dispute regarding the
Letters to Timothy and Titus? Although an exhaustive study of
this question is not possible here, it is necessary to deal with
some of the issues involved, for the attitude which we take toward them is certain to affect our understanding of the message
of these letters for us today.

Any reader of the New Testament will, of course, observe
that First and Second Timothy are clearly marked in the opening verses as having been written by "Paul, an apostle of Christ
Jesus," to Timothy, his son in the faith. The Letter to Titus is
identified in much the same way. There is no question of the
accuracy of the text here. Either the letters were written by
Paul or they were written by one of Paul's followers who published them in Paul's name. As the student of the New Testament reads through the letters themselves he will find that they
contain a considerable amount of biographical material which
is given in the name of Paul. For example, the first chapter of
First Timothy includes a reference to Timothy as Paul's son in
the faith (1:2), a moving biographical passage in which Paul re-
calls his life as a persecutor of the Christian community and
thinks of himself as the chief of sinners (1:12-17), and a reference to the disciplinary action he has taken against Hymenaeus
and Alexander (1:19-20). Other such references appear in 2:7;
3:14-15; and 4:13. Along with these the student should examine
the several personal references to Timothy, such as 5:21, 23;
6:14, 20. Second Timothy is particularly rich in its biographical
material. Consider, for example, in the first chapter the reference
to Timothy's mother and grandmother and to his ordination

(1:5-6), Paul's personal testimony of faith (1:11-12), and the beautiful tribute to Onesiphorus (1:15-18). In similar fashion II Timothy 4:6-18 contains Paul's great statement as he stands at the end of life and looks forward to the crown of righteousness, his comment on the desertion of Demas, a number of personal requests, his mention of his trial in which those of Asia deserted him, and his confidence that the Lord will rescue him from every evil and save him for his eternal Kingdom. Notice also the incidental reference to Trophimus who was left sick at Miletus. The Letter to Titus contains specific directions to Titus concerning his administration of the church in Crete and a number of personal references, including the plans of Paul to spend the winter at Nicopolis (1:5; 3:12-15).

The average reader of the New Testament will accept the Pastoral Epistles as Pauline on the basis of the opening identifications and the biographical references. But the student who examines with some care the Letters to Timothy and the Letter to Titus will realize that there are some unanswered questions.

There is an obvious difference between the language of the Pastoral Epistles and that of Paul's other letters. This is seen more clearly, of course, in the study of the Greek text, but it can also be discerned in the reading of the English translation. A typical example is the use in the Pastorals of the expression "The saying is sure and worthy of full acceptance" (I Tim. 1:15; 3:1; 4:9; II Tim. 2:11; Titus 3:8). This particular expression is not found in the other letters of Paul. Careful studies have shown, moreover, that perhaps a third of the words which are used in the Pastorals are not found in the earlier letters of Paul. And some of the words which are found in both sets of letters are used in the Pastoral Epistles with a somewhat different meaning. For example, the word "righteousness" in the Pastorals describes an ethical quality (I Tim. 6:11; II Tim. 2:22), while in Romans it describes a religious relationship. Such differences in vocabulary between the Pastoral Epistles and Paul's other letters have made careful students wonder whether both sets of letters could have been written by the same person.

Style and Content

A discerning reader of the Pastoral Epistles will also sense differences in style of writing. Such differences move in the realm of intangibles. But generally it is obvious that the Pastoral Epistles move at a more placid and ordered pace than the earlier letters. They abound in long and somewhat tedious passages in condemnation of false teachers (for example, I Tim. 1:3-7; II Tim. 2:14-26; 3:1-9; Titus 1:10-14). There are great passages in the Pastorals which are worthy of Paul at his best, but on the whole they do not seem to have the dash and the fire of the earlier works.

More important than differences in style are differences in content. The student who has studied carefully the Letters to the Thessalonians will feel at once a change in emphasis concerning the expectation of the Lord's return. This expectation is still an important article of faith in the Letters to Timothy and Titus (I Tim. 6:14; II Tim. 4:8; Titus 2:13), but in the Letters to the Thessalonians it is found in almost every chapter and is central to the argument at many places.

In the Pastorals the center of interest seems to have shifted in other ways. The writer is very much concerned with church organization and structure. In First Timothy he lays down in detail the qualifications of elders and deacons. He instructs Titus to appoint elders in every town and gives again his list of qualifications of elders (Titus 1:5-9). Here we have men who are obviously acknowledged as supervisors of the church in the name of the Lord. It is true that a pattern of church discipline had been worked out within the Thessalonian church (I Thess. 5:12:13; II Thess. 3:14-15), but what was incidental in that congregation has become central in the Pastoral Epistles. It is obvious also that these later letters express a doctrine of ordination not set forth with equal clarity in Paul's earlier writings.

The writer of the Pastoral Epistles has a deep concern for the preservation of the purity of the faith, shown in his attacks on false teachers, in his emphasis on sound teaching, and even more in his development of the idea of a "deposit of faith." In the undisputed letters of Paul "faith" is thought of in terms of definite commitment to Jesus as Lord and Savior. This idea is not lacking in the Pastoral Epistles, but the center of interest is more in the preservation of *the* faith. This writer believes that at the heart of Christianity there is a "given." This is defined as a *deposit* which has been received. It must be guarded and it must be passed on to those who will be faithful in the teaching of others (I Tim. 4:6; II Tim. 2:2).

Place in the Life of Paul

Any student of the Pastoral Epistles will face almost immediately the question of their place in the life of Paul. In First Timothy, Paul is a free man who has been in Macedonia. He has instructed Timothy to remain in Ephesus (I Tim. 1:3). He hopes to come to him soon (I Tim. 3:14). In the Letter to Titus, Paul has been in Crete and expects to spend the winter at Nicopolis (Titus 1:5; 3:12). In Second Timothy, Paul is in prison in Rome (II Tim. 1:17). It is obvious that he has not been in prison very long, for he speaks of having left Erastus at Corinth and Trophimus sick at Miletus. He has left a coat with Carpus at Troas. He has had with him in Rome Demas, Crescens, Titus, and Tychicus, but for one reason or another, they have departed. Luke is still with him. Paul has recently had a trial. His friends from Asia have deserted him, but he has been able to give his testimony to the Gentiles. He urges Timothy to come to him (II Tim. 4:9-18).

Can these references be fitted into the story of Paul as told in Acts? There is no difficulty in placing the Letters to the Thessalonians into Luke's story, but the general consensus is that the references in the Pastorals cannot be so fitted into the narrative of Acts.

For this reason those who accept the Pastoral Epistles as Pauline usually combine their position with a reconstruction of the life of Paul, assuming, for example, that he was released from the imprisonment in Rome which is described in Acts, and that he went on another journey in which he visited such places as Crete, Macedonia, and Ephesus. First Timothy and Titus are assigned to this journey and Second Timothy to the imprisonment which followed it. On the other hand, those who reject the Pauline authorship of the Pastorals usually feel that Paul was executed at the end of the Roman imprisonment which Luke describes.

The reader of this commentary is probably ready to ask why the debate is important. The Letter to the Hebrews, for example, was at one time listed among the letters of Paul. Today very few hold that Paul wrote Hebrews. But the message of the Letter to the Hebrews is not affected by the argument about its author. The question in debate in the discussion of the authorship of the Pastoral Epistles is not the question as to whether or not they

are to be accepted as Scripture. Even if these letters came out of
the early part of the second century, they are from the hand of
a devout disciple of Paul who tried to express in his own language what he felt Paul, if he had been alive at that time, would
have said to the men of his generation. The understanding of the
Christian faith which is expressed in these letters has been judged
by the Church to be in harmony with her faith, and the other
letters have been received into the Canon. They come to us with
the authority of Scripture, whether they were written by Paul or
not.

Why, then, is the question of authorship important? In I Timothy 2:5-6 we have the classic statement of the doctrine of Christ
as the one Mediator between God and man. We read: "For there
is one God, and there is one mediator between God and men, the
man Christ Jesus, who gave himself as a ransom for all, the testimony to which was borne at the proper time." This statement
is true whether it was written by Paul around A.D. 68 or by a
disciple of his a few decades later. But when we come to verse 7
we read: "For this I was appointed a preacher and apostle (I am
telling the truth, I am not lying), a teacher of the Gentiles in
faith and truth." Here the question of authorship *is* important.
In the interpretation of this verse it does make a difference
whether we think of it as a genuine testimony from Paul himself
or consider it a statement deemed appropriate to Paul but made
by a disciple who wrote in the name of Paul some years after
his death. And, in a limited sense, the authority of the doctrinal
statement is affected by our decision concerning the authorship
of verse 7. In I Timothy 1:12-17 there is a biographical passage
containing the great statement: "The saying is sure and worthy
of full acceptance, that Christ Jesus came into the world to save
sinners." We will all approve of this statement regardless of our
theories concerning its authorship. But the writer continues:
"And I am the foremost of sinners." (He is thinking here of his
activity as the persecutor of the Church which he has mentioned
in verse 13.) He goes on to say that in showing mercy to him
Jesus Christ displayed "his perfect patience for an example to
those who were to believe in him for eternal life." In an auto-
biographical passage of this kind the question of authorship is
crucial for interpretation.

It does, therefore, become necessary for a writer of a commentary on the Pastoral Epistles to state the point of view from

which his commentary is written. This commentary is written on the assumption that First and Second Timothy and Titus are Pauline. Some explanation, of course, needs to be offered for the changes in vocabulary and doctrinal emphasis which have already been considered. No complete answer can be given to the problems; they remain in part unsolved for anyone who accepts the Pauline authorship. But some suggestions can be made. A period of around fifteen years lies between the earlier letters of Paul and the Pastoral Epistles. In this period Paul could have made changes in his vocabulary. The difference in vocabulary could also be explained by a change in the persons who actually transcribed the letters. Paul dictated his letters, signing them at the end for identification. In composing the Pastoral Epistles, he may have outlined his ideas and allowed considerable freedom to his secretary in the actual writing. It is also possible that these are genuine letters of Paul which were expanded in places by a disciple, some years after Paul's death. In this case there would be no way to distinguish between the portions that were actually written by Paul and those which were added later. We would still have to interpret the letters as Pauline.

While there are problems involved in holding to the Pauline authorship of the Pastorals which should not be ignored, these difficulties may not be so great as those which are involved in an attempt to explain the origin of these letters on any other basis. There are, moreover, good reasons for holding to the Pauline authorship, among them the identification of the author in the opening sentences and the biographical material in the letters themselves. Such clear testimony is not to be brushed aside lightly. To be considered also is the almost unanimous opinion of the Church through the first eighteen hundred years of her existence. One early writer, Marcion, rejected them, but he did so on doctrinal grounds. With this one exception they are consistently accepted and quoted as Pauline by the writers of the Early Church. When we remember the care with which Paul identified his letters, we must realize that it would not have been easy for letters written some time after Paul's death to gain unquestioned acceptance as Pauline. Much weight should also be given to the testimony of the great commentators of a generation or more ago, who, although sympathetic to the critical approach to Scripture, decided for the Pauline authorship on the basis of examination of the evidence. Against their testimony we must recognize the fact that the majority of New Testament scholars today do not hold to the Pauline authorship of the Pastoral Epistles. But there is still a respectable body of scholars who believe that these letters were written by Paul, and a much larger group of scholars who feel that they contain genuine Pauline material.

Many readers of the Pastoral Epistles will find themselves drawn to accept the Pauline authorship because of their feeling that the biographical portions of the letters are genuine. Who would invent the unique tribute to Onesiphorous (II Tim. 1: 15-18), or the advice to Timothy to take a little wine for the sake of his stomach and his frequent ailments? (I Tim. 5:23). This feeling concerning the genuineness of the biographical material comes with particular force in the study of Second Timothy. The picture which this letter gives of the great Apostle in his last imprisonment has the ring of authenticity. Some of Paul's friends have deserted him. Others have been sent on dangerous missions. Only Luke is with him. He has had one trial which he has turned into an opportunity to witness to his Lord. He knows the end is near, and he yearns to see Timothy before his death. Read, in this connection, II Timothy 4:6-8. Can one fail to be moved by this testimony? Read the account of the trial (II Tim. 4:16-17) and then hear Paul say: "The Lord will rescue me from every evil and save me for his heavenly kingdom" (vs. 18). Can one fail to feel that this is Paul's final word to Timothy and through him to the Church?

The problems associated with an acceptance of Pauline authorship are real but they need not be decisive. There is a variation in language, but men use different vocabularies in varying situations and at different stages of their development. There is a shift in emphasis, but this is to be expected as Paul grows old and as the return of Christ seems to be delayed. The interest in the organization of the Church is not unnatural for a man who must soon leave the scene of his earthly activity. In a similar way the deepening concern for the purity of the gospel and for the deposit of faith is appropriate to the situation which Paul would have faced when these letters were written. Moreover, the assumption of two Roman imprisonments is almost necessary, considering the difference in Paul's attitude to his imprisonment in Colossians and Philemon and in Second Timothy.

OUTLINE

First Timothy

A Good Conscience and Genuine Faith. I Timothy 1:1-20
Directions for Public Worship. I Timothy 2:1—3:13
How to Behave in the Church. I Timothy 3:14—6:21

Second Timothy

The Gospel of God. II Timothy 1:1-18
The Faithful Christian Pastor. II Timothy 2:1-26
A Charge to Timothy. II Timothy 3:1-17
Paul's Farewell Message. II Timothy 4:1-22

Titus

Greetings, Including a Summary of the Gospel. Titus 1:1-4
Instructions for Titus' Ministry in Crete. Titus 1:5—3:11
Final Instructions and Greetings. Titus 3:12-15

COMMENTARY

A GOOD CONSCIENCE AND GENUINE FAITH

I Timothy 1:1-20

Greetings (1:1-2)

The Letters of Paul to Timothy are written with the authority of "an apostle of Christ Jesus." Paul does not mention his apostleship in the Letters to the Thessalonians, perhaps because they were written as coming from him, Silas, and Timothy. It would be the gracious thing for him not to use at this time a title which, in its strictest sense, could not be applied to his associates. Timothy also joins Paul in the Letter to the Philippians, where Paul refers to himself and Timothy as "servants of Christ Jesus." In the personal Letter to Philemon he speaks of himself as "a prisoner for Christ Jesus," and Timothy is mentioned as associated with him in the letter. In all of his other letters, Paul asserts his apostleship. It is on the basis of his authority as Apostle that he gives Timothy instructions for his work as a pastor. Moreover, he is an Apostle "by command of God our Savior and of Christ Jesus our hope." God and Christ Jesus are associated here as both responsible for the apostleship which Paul has received. God is called "our Savior." The word is frequently used to describe the work of Jesus, but it properly applies to the redemption which God wrought out through Jesus Christ.

The letter is directed to Timothy, whom Paul calls "my true child in the faith." Timothy joined Paul and Silas as an attendant on the second missionary journey. We learn from Acts that his mother was a Jewess and his father a Greek. He was probably converted by Paul on the first missionary journey. When Paul took Timothy with him on the second missionary journey he insisted that Timothy be circumcised to avoid the criticisms of the Jews (Acts 16:1-3). In writing to the Philippians, he commends Timothy to them as he says: "I have no one like him, who will be genuinely anxious for your welfare. They all look after their own interests, not those of Jesus Christ. But Timothy's worth you know, how as a son with a father he has served with me in the gospel" (Phil. 2:20-22). In the Second Letter to Timothy, Paul is deeply concerned lest Timothy falter in the time of persecution. Probably the latest reference to Timothy in the New Testament is one made by the author of the Letter to the Hebrews in his closing paragraph: "You should understand that our brother Timothy has been released, with whom I shall see you if he comes soon." We would judge from this that Timothy has been in prison, that he has been released, and that he and the writer of the Letter to the Hebrews plan a visit together to the Christians to whom this letter is directed. When Paul in the First Letter to Timothy calls him "my true child in the faith" he gives expression to the intimacy of his relation to Timothy and also to his confidence in Timothy's understanding of the meaning of the Christian faith. In the closing sentence of the introduction, Paul adds "mercy" to the usual prayer for "grace" and "peace." He does this also in the introduction to Second Timothy, but not in the Letter to Titus.

Against the False Teachers (1:3-7)

When Paul was going into Macedonia he urged Timothy to remain in Ephesus. We should like to know whether or not Paul got to Macedonia. We should also like to know whether, if he reached Macedonia, he was able to visit again the church at Thessalonica. No doubt many changes had taken place in this church in the period of around fifteen years between the Letters to the Thessalonians and this Letter to Timothy. But there is no answer to these questions. The fact that Timothy was urged to stay in Ephesus would suggest that Timothy was somewhat reluctant to accept the assignment. He was left at Ephesus in order that he might deal with the danger of false teaching at this great metropolitan center in Asia. Timothy was to charge certain persons not to teach "any different doctrine." Thus at the beginning there appears an emphasis on sound doctrine which runs through the entire letter. There is nothing new in this. In all of his letters Paul is concerned to see that his churches have a true understanding of the Christian faith. He proclaims a doctrine which has been entrusted to him and which he is not at liberty to change. But as the Church became more deeply rooted in the culture of the Greek world, it became increasingly necessary to strive for purity of doctrine. Christian teachers would be tempted to soften the demands of the gospel so as to make it more acceptable to their audience, or to seek to find in the gospel support for pagan ideas which were quite foreign to its inner meaning. Every age is presented with the problem of preserving the purity of the gospel message and at the same time of interpreting that message in a way that is relevant to the needs of the time.

Timothy was also to charge these teachers not to occupy themselves with "myths and endless genealogies which promote speculations." The exact nature of these myths and endless genealogies is unknown. The reference to the Law, which follows a little later, would suggest a group of Christians of Jewish background who were still absorbed in some of the endless disputes of the rabbis. At any rate, a besetting sin of Christian teachers in all ages is to become interested in debates and discussions which have little or no relevance to life. Christian teachers can give themselves endlessly to the trivial, the unimportant, and the irrelevant. They can become absorbed in speculative questions which have no real bearing on Christian thought and life. In condemning this sort of thing in Ephesus, Paul is speaking also to Christian teachers in any generation. The real danger is that such absorption can become a substitute for the proclamation of the gospel which calls forth faith. This is what Paul means when he says that these teachers are becoming absorbed in speculations rather than "the divine training that is in faith." The Greek words which are translated "divine training" can be literally translated "the dispensation of God." Paul is concerned that all Christian teachers should be absorbed only in the understanding of the dispensation of God which is given to us in the Christian faith.

Verse 5 gives the charge that the true Christian pastor is to have as his aim, "love that issues from a pure heart and a good conscience and sincere faith." The proclamation of the gospel should, in the end, produce love between man and man. This Christian love is rooted in man's response to the love of God in Christ. Such love flows from a pure heart, a good conscience, and sincere faith. Christian teaching should lead to purity of heart, to right conduct in which a man lives in harmony with the demands of a sensitive conscience, and to deep and genuine Christian convictions as the true foundation for Christian living.

Paul returns to his description of certain persons at Ephesus who do not meet his ideal for the good teacher. These persons have turned aside from any real concern with the pure heart, the good conscience, or the genuine Christian conviction. In so doing they have wandered away into empty discussions which are not profitable for Christian living. Furthermore, they desire to be teachers of the Law but do not understand the full implications of what they are saying and do not have a true understanding of the subject.

The Place of the Law (1:8-11)

The problem of the Christian attitude to the Law is always with us. In the first period of Paul's ministry he had to deal with the Judaizers, Christian Jews who insisted that, in addition to their profession of faith in Jesus Christ, all Gentiles should be required to receive circumcision and to keep the Law of Moses as the conditions of salvation. Paul's first great controversy centered in his effort to hold the Christian Church to the response of faith as the only condition of salvation. It was here that he developed his great doctrine of justification by faith alone. He deals with this issue in Romans and in Galatians. The false teachers in Ephesus are not accused of being Judaizers. They were not insisting on circumcision and obedience to the Law of Moses as conditions of salvation, but they did not understand the proper place of the Law in the life of the Christian.

Paul does not disparage the Law. He knows that the Law is necessary to bring conviction of sin; it is for "the disobedient." There follows a long list of sins that are obviously condemned by the Law, sins which would, of course, be condemned in any code of ethics. Men should be warned that the wrath of God rests on those who are guilty of such sins as those listed in verses 9-10. But it is not proclaiming the gospel to put as the center of preaching the Law and its penalties. We are proclaiming the gospel when we give our witness to Jesus Christ and ask men to accept the offer of salvation which God has made through him. When men have done this they come into a new relation to God, and the true basis of ethical appeal to them becomes the charge to live in a manner which is worthy of the high calling in Christ Jesus. This was Paul's appeal to the Thessalonians, and an understanding of it enables us to know what he means when he says that the Law is good if we use it in the right manner. We will not reach the Christian goal of love from a pure heart and a good conscience and genuine faith by dealing with the penalties and threats of the Law. We will reach this goal only as we call men to respond to the glorious gospel of the blessed God with which we have been entrusted.

Entrusted with the Gospel (1:12-17)

During the whole of his ministry as a Christian preacher, Paul had a profound sense of the high privilege which was his in being called to proclaim the good news of Jesus Christ. He writes to the Ephesians: "To me, though I am the very least of all the saints, this grace was given, to preach to the Gentiles the unsearchable riches of Christ" (Eph. 3:8). In the present passage he lifts his heart in thanksgiving to Christ Jesus who has accounted him faithful and appointed him to his service. In verse 12 he probably has in mind not only his original call, received on the road to Damascus, but also his summons to Antioch received through Barnabas, and the call to carry the gospel to the Gentiles which came to him at Antioch (Acts 9:1-22; 11:19-26; 13:1-3). When Paul stood before King Agrippa he could say: "I was not disobedient to the heavenly vision" (Acts 26:19). It is one thing to receive a vision and another to be faithful to it through life. Paul's sense of wonder and thanksgiving is deepened by his knowledge of what he had been before God saved him and called him to be his messenger. He remembers his early activity as the persecutor of the Church. In the Revised Standard Version verse 13 reads: "though I formerly blasphemed and persecuted and insulted him." A more literal translation of the Greek is: "though I was before a blasphemer, and a persecutor, and injurious (or a doer of outrage)." Of course it is true that Jesus is identified with his Church. At the time of Paul's conversion Jesus said to him: "Saul, Saul, why do you persecute *me?*" (Acts 9:4).

When Paul speaks of himself as a blasphemer he does not mean that he was a profane man. In describing to King Agrippa his activity as a persecutor of the Christians he says: "I punished them often in all the synagogues and tried to make them blaspheme" (Acts 26:11). Here "blaspheme" has the technical meaning of denying that Jesus is Lord; that is, repudiating the Christian faith. Paul had belonged to those who rejected the claim of Jesus to be the Christ. In the last phrase, "doer of outrage," Paul refers to the violence which he had done to the first followers of Jesus. He had arrested them and put them in prison. Some of them had been put to death with his approval. It is the lot of the religious persecutor to be forced to do in the name of his service to God crimes of violence which offend his finer feelings.

As persecutor Paul was motivated by religious faith. He thought he was doing a service to God in attempting to stamp out what to him was a distortion of Jewish faith. (Accounts of Paul's activity as the persecutor of the Church are found in Acts 8:3; 9:1-3; 22:4-5, 19-20; 26:9-11; I Corinthians 15:9; Galatians 1:13, 22-23.)

Paul's persecution of the Church was carried on in ignorance and in unbelief. As a persecutor, he was acting consistently with his conviction. He saw the full implications of the Christian faith as set forth by Stephen (Acts 7). And he knew that Stephen's ideas would be destructive of Judaism as he understood it. Paul's unbelief was sinful. He had hardened his heart against the witness to Jesus which he must have received from Stephen and others. The amazing thing to Paul was that God had come to him in the midst of his sin and unbelief and had called him to become his messenger to the Gentiles. It was where sin had abounded that grace had much more abounded. Paul the sinner had found himself the object of the grace and the love of Christ Jesus. In writing to the Romans he said: "God shows his love for us in that while we were yet sinners Christ died for us" (Rom. 5:8). In that statement he was thinking in general terms of the love of God which, at great cost, wrought out a way of redemption for sinful men. But in I Timothy 1:14, he is thinking in personal terms of the infinite love which came to him when he was on his way to Damascus to persecute the Church. Against the background of his understanding of the gospel, and out of the depths of his personal experience, Paul makes a statement which he says is sure and worthy of full acceptance: "Christ Jesus came into the world to save sinners." The statement implies the pre-existence of Christ. The classic expression of this doctrine is in Philippians 2:6-11. In Jesus, he who has always existed in terms of equality with God enters our world. But the implications in terms of the Person of Christ are incidental to the statement that Christ Jesus came into our world *to save sinners*. Paul remembers the way in which Christ came to him as Savior, the way the love of God in Christ reached down to save him in his mad career as the persecutor of the Church of Christ.

It is in such a setting that Paul calls himself "the foremost of sinners." This does not mean that even in his career as a persecutor Paul was the worst man who ever lived. At the time he was a deeply religious man, with a noble personal code of ethics. We may be sure that he had never been guilty of the sins listed in verses 9-10. But in some ways Paul the persecutor was a much more dangerous man than men who lived for the sins of the flesh. If Paul had had his will as a persecutor, the Church of Christ would have been blotted out before it had time to root itself in the life of man. And the loss to all mankind would have been incalculable. We know that the Church was in Christ's keeping and that Paul could not prevail, but we must not fail to understand the implications of Paul's effort to destroy it. The miracle of grace was that Christ came to the persecutor, not in destructive judgment, but in love and mercy. It was not until after he became a Christian that Paul saw the full iniquity of his course as a persecutor. We know the depth of our iniquity only as we know that our sins are forgiven. As Paul looks back on his experience of justification he feels that the "perfect patience" of Jesus Christ has been set forth in his case as an example to all who are to believe in Christ for eternal life. Those who persist in such sins as those listed in verses 9-10 are certain to experience the wrath of God; but no man, regardless of how deep in sin he is, need despair. Christ Jesus came into the world to save sinners. This word declares the gospel to each sinner, proclaiming that Christ Jesus came to save *him*. The forgiveness of God is available for him if he will receive it. The God who saved Paul the persecutor is ready to save all who will repent and look to him in faith. We have an echo here of the words of Jesus: "I have not come to call the righteous, but sinners to repentance" (Luke 5:32).

Jesus promises eternal life to those who believe in him. Eternal life is, first of all, a *quality* of life. It is the life of those who have come to know that in Christ their sins are forgiven and they stand in a new relation to God. The experience of salvation, however, always carries with it also the hope of eternal life in the world to come. It is in the proclamation of this gospel that men are led into a new community in which they come to know the love that proceeds from a pure heart and a good conscience and sincere faith.

As Paul contemplates the full sweep of the gospel which he has experienced, he bursts forth in the doxology: "To the King of ages, immortal, invisible, the only God, be honor and glory for ever and ever." The God who has saved Paul is the God of every age, including our own. This God is immortal. He can never cease to exist. He is invisible. We cannot lay hold of him by physical eyes. He is the *only* God. There is no God beside him. This statement prepares the way for the statement of the unity of God made in the next chapter. The doxology closes with the ascription of glory and honor to the God who has come to men in Jesus Christ.

The Good Warfare (1:18-20)

The charge which is committed to Timothy (vs. 18) is not defined. It probably refers to the instructions given to Timothy in the beginning of the chapter. He was to charge certain persons at Ephesus not to teach a different doctrine, or to become absorbed in myths and endless genealogies, or to attempt to teach the Law without understanding the true place of the Law in Christian teaching. We can be sure that Paul was also thinking of the more positive charge to proclaim the gospel in such a way that it would call forth faith and love. The reference to "the prophetic utterances" must be to certain predictions which had been made by Christian prophets concerning the usefulness of Timothy in the ministry of the gospel. If a man knows that Christian leaders have made strong predictions about his fitness for the ministry, he is apt to be inspired to seek to fulfill their expectations. Timothy knows the predictions that have been made concerning him. Inspired by these he is to wage the good warfare. In Second Timothy, Paul says of himself, "I have fought the good fight" (II Tim. 4:7). The reference is to the good fight of faith. All of life has about it an element of struggle, but it makes a great deal of difference whether one fights on the right or the wrong side.

In waging the good warfare, Timothy must be careful to hold to faith and a good conscience. The word "faith" probably refers to the content of Christian doctrine, especially the meaning of the life, death, and resurrection of Jesus Christ which Timothy has found at the heart of the Christian community. But the idea of faith as personal surrender to Jesus Christ as Lord is not excluded. Without such faith it is impossible to live as a Christian. The loss of faith means the loss of the foundation for Christian living. But in waging the good warfare a good conscience is also necessary. The word "conscience" designates the capacity to distinguish between right and wrong. We hold on to a good conscience when we consistently seek to do what we know is right.

Against the background of this charge to Timothy, an interesting reference is made to two men named Hymenaeus and Alexander. It would seem that these men had been members of the Christian community but had lived in violation of their consciences. We do not know what they had done, but we do know that they had rejected the voice of conscience. Having rejected conscience, they made shipwreck of their faith. We all know that when we fail to heed the promptings of conscience we can blunt its witness. If we habitually get up when we hear an alarm clock, we are not apt to fail to hear it. But if we habitually ignore it, we may find that the sound of the alarm eventually fails to awaken us. In similar manner, if we heed the compunctions of conscience we find that we grow in our capacity to discern between right and wrong. If we consistently violate our conscience we may cease to be sensitive to moral issues. But Paul gave this line of thinking a different turn. These men, by rejecting conscience, "made shipwreck of their faith." Every man must seek in some measure to justify himself. When a man who has professed the Christian faith persists in living in a way that he knows is wrong, he is apt to begin to have doubts about his faith. If he is going to ignore the Ten Commandments he will prefer not to think of them as a summary of a moral law which expresses the will of God for man. A breakdown in a man's morals leads to uncertainty about his basic convictions. There is a double movement here. Our deeds are the expression of our creeds, and a breakdown in faith may be followed by disintegration in morals. But it is equally true that the loss of a good conscience may lead to the shipwreck of faith.

Paul has delivered these men to Satan that they might learn not to blaspheme. As is the case with Paul's assertion that he was at one time a blasphemer (1:13), the reference here is probably to the denial of Jesus as Lord. Hymenaeus and Alexander first suffered a breakdown in morals. By rejecting conscience they made shipwreck of their faith. The breakdown of faith led to blasphemy, so that instead of saying, "Jesus is Lord," they said, "Jesus be cursed!" (see I Cor. 12:3 for the two phrases). The full meaning of the phrase "delivered to Satan" is unknown. It may point to expulsion from the Christian community. When men turn from Christ, they come under the power of evil. When Hymenaeus and Alexander ceased to serve the Christ, they began to serve the evil one. But Paul hopes that their experiences in the way of evil may lead them to the place of repentance and new obedience. He hopes that they may learn *not* to blaspheme. The way of the transgressor is hard, and many of those who walk in it for a time turn from it to acknowledge again Jesus as Lord.

DIRECTIONS FOR PUBLIC WORSHIP
I Timothy 2:1—3:13

Prayers for All Men (2:1-7)

The emphasis in chapter 2 turns to more specific directions concerning the worship of the Church, including prayers that are to be made for all men. The words in 2:1 describe different aspects of prayer, such as supplication, intercession, and thanksgiving, but the emphasis of the sentence is on the desire that prayers be made for *all* men.

As a specific illustration of the prayers that are to be made for all men, "kings and all who are in high positions" are mentioned. Prayers are to be made for rulers, in the hope that God's people may be permitted to "lead a quiet and peaceable life, godly and respectful in every way." Those who are in positions of great authority are often called upon to make decisions which affect the destinies of thousands of people. Rulers hold in their hands decisions which make for war or peace. The men who sit on the boards of great corporations make decisions that may determine the economic well-being of large areas of the earth. Those who are charged with this kind of responsibility are human. They are subjected to tremendous pressures, and they make mistakes. Christians should pray for them. The call to prayer for kings and all who are in high positions shows that the Christian community is never to be thought of as opposing a government which makes responsible use of its powers.

In verses 3 and 4 the principle that prayers should be made for all men (including kings and those in high positions) is supported by the fact that the making of such prayers is good and acceptable in the sight of God our Savior since he "desires all men to be saved and to come to the knowledge of the truth." In public or in private worship we should take care to make only those prayers which we feel are acceptable to God. But here is one prayer we can confidently make. In saying that God "de-

sires all men to be saved," Paul does not mean that all men will
be saved. God has given a limited amount of freedom to humans.
They have freedom enough to make decisions but not freedom
enough to escape the consequences of their decisions. In particular, God does not violate the personalities of men when they are
confronted with the decision concerning Jesus Christ. Paul is
not dealing here with the extent to which God's offer of forgiveness in Jesus Christ will be accepted. He is simply stating that
the saving purpose of God reaches to all men. The statement of
this truth about God, moreover, does not in any way destroy
the concept of the wrath of God. The judge who administers
punishment may do so because he knows that punishment is
deserved. He may at the same time hope that the offender will
see the error of his ways and return to right thinking and right
living.

The fact that the God who is our Savior desires all men to be
saved, however, does cut across any idea that the God who has
come to us in Christ is in a peculiar sense the God of any racial
or class or national group. There is no place here for the concept
of a tribal God.

The knowledge of the truth which God desires that all men
should have is now defined. "There is one God" (vs. 5). There
is a close connection between the statement that there is one God
and the idea that this one God desires all men to be saved. If
there is only one God, then this one God must be the God
of all men. The great prophets knew this (for example, Isa.
45:21-23).

If we believe that there is only one God, we must at once ask
where this one God has made himself known. Paul's answer to
this necessary question is in the affirmation, "There is one mediator between God and men, the man Christ Jesus, who gave himself as a ransom for all." Christians, Jews, and Muslims can unite
in saying that there is only one God. They divide, however, when
they say where this one God has revealed himself. The Muslim
would say: "There is no God but Allah," and would add, "Mu-
hammad is his prophet." The Jews find the revelation of God in
the Scriptures of Israel, recounting the great events of their history interpreted by their prophets as the spokesmen of God. But
Christians insist that "there is one mediator between God and
men, the man Christ Jesus." It is as the God-man that Christ
Jesus is Mediator. He came into the world to save sinners. He

was born of a woman. He was born under the Law. He entered into the total range of our human experiences. He is at the same time God and man.

Jesus is the one Mediator in that he gave himself as a ransom for all. He reveals God to man, not by setting forth certain ideas about God, but by a tremendous deed in which he gives himself as a ransom for us all. It is in the death of the Christ for us that God shows his love for us. It is in the death of the Mediator that we feel the full force of God's wrath against sin. In Jesus the one God has come to us in the context of our earthly life and made himself known to us as the God who desires all men to be saved and to come to the knowledge of the truth.

If the one God makes himself known through a person who appears at a definite time and place in history, it is necessary that testimony be borne to all men concerning the significance of this event (vs. 6). We have here, of course, a tremendous paradox: the knowledge which is needed for my soul's salvation comes to me through an event in history which is testified to in a book. But this paradox of Christianity cannot be avoided. The gospel is good news. It starts with that which God has done in Christ, and it proclaims the understanding of the significance of the work of Christ which God has committed to his Church.

To affirm that there is one Mediator between God and men, the man Christ Jesus, is to lay the foundation for the intolerance that is at the heart of Christianity. A Christian can appreciate the good that is found in other religions, and a Christian should respect the convictions of those who hold to other faiths. But Christians cannot surrender the conviction that Jesus Christ is in a unique sense the one Mediator between God and men. Emphasis on Christ as the *one* Mediator leads also to the idea of the finality of Christianity. The God who has sent a prophet may send another prophet. But the God who has made himself known in a unique deed, in which the God-man gives himself as a ransom for men, cannot repeat this deed. There will not be another mediator to give a more adequate revelation of God.

The discussion of the work of Christ as Mediator is closed by a reminder of Paul's own appointment as a witness to Jesus Christ (vs. 7). The beginning of the testimony to Jesus Christ took place before Paul became a Christian. But in a peculiar sense he was called to carry to the great Gentile world the knowledge of the salvation which God had prepared for all mankind.

The significance of Paul is that always he points beyond himself to the man Christ Jesus, who is the one Mediator between God and men.

The Place of Woman in Worship (2:8-15)

The treatment which is given here to the place of woman in worship presents certain difficulties of interpretation in relation to the relevance of the passage for the life of the Church in the modern world. (For background concerning the New Testament teaching, the reader should examine I Corinthians 11:2-16; 14: 33-36; Galatians 3:28; Ephesians 5:21-33; Colossians 3:18; and I Peter 3:1-6.) The passage on the one Mediator (2:5-7) is incidental to the movement of Paul's thought as a whole. It was given to support his position that prayers should be made for all men. Verse 8 returns to the discussion of public worship. The reference to the "men" as they lead in prayer introduces some comments on the place of woman in public worship. While the comments here may have some general reference, they are directed primarily to the behavior of women in the worship of the congregation. When they come to worship the women should adorn themselves modestly and sensibly, in seemly apparel. Most Christians would agree, although they might not agree on just what is involved in dressing "modestly and sensibly in seemly apparel." Paul spells out his meaning by saying, "not with braided hair or gold or pearls or costly attire." Again, most would agree that extravagance and display in dress should be avoided at all times, but particularly in public worship. Women are encouraged to adorn themselves "by good deeds, as befits women who profess religion." That women can make themselves most attractive by their good deeds is also a matter of general agreement. In a parallel passage, Peter writes to the women: "Let not yours be the outward adorning with braiding of hair, decoration of gold, and wearing of robes, but let it be the hidden person of the heart with the imperishable jewel of a gentle and quiet spirit, which in God's sight is very precious" (I Peter 3:3-4). We are true to the spirit of these passages when we say that the dress of Christians at public worship should be marked by simplicity and taste. It does not follow that the church should attempt by specific rules to regulate the dress of her members.

Paul's suggestions for the dress of women at public worship can be interpreted in terms that are meaningful in the life of the

Church today. The real problem in the passage comes in verses 11-12: "Let a woman learn in silence with all submissiveness. I permit no woman to teach or to have authority over men; she is to keep silent" (see also I Cor. 14:33-36). This position is supported by an appeal to the Creation, where Adam was formed first and then Eve, and also to the Fall, in which the woman was deceived and became a transgressor of the divine command. In attempting to understand this practice of the Church in Paul's day, we should remember the accepted subordination of woman to man in the whole of the ancient world. This was true among both Jews and Gentiles. The emancipation of woman has come about through the impact of the insights of the Christian faith on the orders of society in the non-Christian world. Paul himself was not without a more radical approach to the place of woman in the Christian society. In Galatians he writes: "In Christ Jesus you are all sons of God, through faith. For as many of you as were baptized into Christ have put on Christ . . . there is neither male nor female; for you are all one in Christ Jesus" (Gal. 3:26-28). Woman occupied a place of dignity and responsibility in the Christian Church of Paul's world. We think, for example, of Lydia, the first convert to Christ in Europe; of Phoebe, whom Paul commends as "our sister" (Rom. 16:1); and of Priscilla, whom Paul calls his fellow worker in Christ (Rom. 16:3).

Not everything that was done in the Church of the New Testament is normative for the Church in all ages. If we are to keep that which is permanent and abiding in the message of Paul, we must learn to discriminate between ideas which are based on things that do not change and ideas which are an adaptation to a local and temporary situation. We are in harmony with the deepest thinking of Paul when we say that a woman should not be disqualified from service in the Church on the basis of her sex.

In the closing comment of this discussion, Paul properly emphasizes the responsibility of woman in bearing children. This responsibility is rooted in the structure of woman's being, and in many ways she finds her fulfillment in it. But the peculiar responsibility of woman, which moves in the sphere of motherhood, does not destroy the great insight that in Christ the division of sex is transcended, and men and women stand together in the Christian community as children of God through faith.

Qualifications of Church Officers (3:1-13)

All Christians should be concerned with the proper organization and government of the Church, and it is natural that this concern should have a prominent place in the Pastoral Epistles. They were written to instruct men who were actively engaged in the supervision of the work of the Church. Some suggestions about the organization of the Church are given at various places in the New Testament. We have the appointment of the seven in Acts 6:1-6. They are not called deacons, but they were appointed to relieve the Apostles of the task of "serving tables," and many think that the office of the deacon goes back to this precedent. Before Paul and Barnabas left for Antioch at the close of the first missionary journey, they appointed elders in every church (Acts 14:23). On his way to Jerusalem, Paul asked for the elders of the church at Ephesus to meet him at Miletus. It is clear that they constituted a recognized body of officers of the congregation (Acts 20:17). The laying on of hands in public recognition of a call to special service is indicated in the fact that the leaders of the church at Antioch consecrated Paul and Barnabas to the work to which the Holy Spirit had called them (Acts 13:1-3). The beginnings of Church government are indicated in the Letters to the Thessalonians (I Thess. 5:12-13; II Thess. 3:14). Similarly, in the greetings of the Letter to the Philippians, Paul mentions both bishops and deacons (Phil. 1:1).

There are four words which are used to describe church officers. They are "apostle," "bishop," "presbyter," and "deacon." In their root meanings, an apostle is one who is sent; a bishop is an overseer or supervisor; a presbyter is an elder, a man of some age; and a deacon is a minister or servant. All of these words are used in earlier parts of the New Testament without any established consistency of meaning. But by the time the Pastorals were written their significance had become more clearly fixed. While the word "apostle" is sometimes used in a broader sense, it is usually limited to the special ministry of the twelve Apostles and Paul. In the development of the history of the Church, the word "bishop" soon came to carry with it a sense of authority greater than that committed to the "elder," but in the Pastorals the words are used interchangeably to describe the same office (see Titus 1:5, 7 and also I Tim. 5:17). The office of deacon seems to have dealt particularly with the administration of relief within the Christian fellowship. Since the early Christian churches were closely knit communities, in which those in need were cared for as the responsibility of the Church as a whole, the deacons often carried heavy obligations and at times had to administer discipline. In many denominations the idea of the deacon as appointed to relieve the Apostles has been extended in the custom of committing to deacons the major responsibility for the care of church property and the handling of the finances of the church.

The qualifications of the bishop as given in I Timothy 3:1-7 deal mainly in traits of character rather than in the development of skills. While there are shades of meaning in the various Greek words used to describe the bishop, or elder, which are not caught in the translation, the Revised Standard Version rendering of the passage is satisfactory and it is not necessary to comment on each word. There are various ways of understanding the phrase "the husband of one wife," but probably the most satisfactory is to take it in its literal sense. It does not mean that a man who is not married cannot be an elder. It does mean that an elder cannot have two wives. When we consider the pagan background of many of the converts to the early Christian churches, we can understand the wisdom of this advice. The churches have never felt that this expression disqualified a man who had married again after the death of his wife. The qualifications of both elders and deacons emphasize the importance of a man's being able to manage his own household. Success in the more limited area of the home is an indication of ability to handle successfully the government of the church. Paul advises against making a man who is a recent convert an elder. Such a man may be puffed up with conceit and fall into the condemnation of the Devil. The reference to the Devil is based on the tradition that the Devil fell through pride. Men should be given a chance to develop in the Christian faith before they are trusted with the honor and the responsibility of the eldership. It would be obvious that in new churches, in which most or all of the members were recent converts, this prohibition would at times have to be relaxed. In certain situations it would also be better to carry on in some form of temporary organization than to exalt to the office of the elder, men who are not yet ready for it. There is wisdom also in the insistence on the selection as elders of men who are well thought of by those outside of the congregation. This gives standing to the church in the life of the community.

In listing the qualifications of the deacon, Paul writes, "not addicted to much wine." Verse 3 in the Revised Standard Version has the expression "no drunkard." In earlier English translations the expression was "not given to wine." Out of the contrast between "not given to wine" and "not given to much wine," there arose the tradition that the elder must not use *any* wine and the deacon must not use *much* wine. But this particular interpretation has no foundation. The best rendering of the Greek word is "not quarrelsome over wine."

The deacons are to hold the mystery of the faith with a clear conscience. The best interpretation of the term "the mystery of the faith" is found in the exposition of the mystery of religion at the close of chapter 3. When a man says he has a "clear conscience," he means that he is not conscious of being involved in the things he knows are wrong. Here again is the emphasis of this epistle on faith and a good conscience. With the deacons, as with the elders, it is wise for men to be tested in the life of the church before they are trusted with the particular responsibilities involved in the work of their office.

The expression in verse 11, "the women," is sometimes understood as referring to the wives of the deacons. It is well, of course, for the men who are selected as deacons to have good wives who will support them in their work. But the sentence probably refers not to the wives of the deacons but to women serving as deacons. We do not know whether they served with the men or in a separate organization, but we can be reasonably sure that there were women in the Pauline churches who served as deaconesses. Phoebe was a deaconess of the church at Cenchreae (Rom. 16:1). This is an example of the way in which women were given places of dignity and responsibility in the world Church of Paul's day.

The office of bishop or elder is described as "a noble task" (vs. 1). In similar fashion, the comment on the work of the deacons is closed: "Those who serve well as deacons gain a good standing for themselves and also great confidence in the faith which is in Christ Jesus" (I Tim. 3:13). Those who have been faithful in the work of the deacon gain standing in the Christian community and their work may prepare them for increasing boldness in the proclamation of the gospel.

HOW TO BEHAVE IN THE CHURCH

I Timothy 3:14—6:21

The Church as Witness to the Truth (3:14-16)

In this passage Paul starts off by making a comparatively simple comment on his purpose in writing, but then he moves from one idea to another until he gives us a remarkable statement of the great mystery which is at the heart of the Christian faith. To his word that he hopes to join Timothy in Ephesus, he adds the comment that he is writing these things in order that, if he is delayed, the Christians at Ephesus may know how they ought to behave in the family of God. This statement sums up the purpose of the letter. It is descriptive of what has already been written and gives unity to the comments that will be made.

The believing community is the household, or family, of God. The Christians in Ephesus are the community which the living God has called into being as his Church. Paul then proceeds at once to define the Church as "the pillar and bulwark of the truth." There is no clear distinction between the words "pillar" and "bulwark"; both point to the function of the Church as the witness to the truth. But Paul's attention has now been caught by the word "truth." In the effort to define what he means by the truth he remarks: "Great indeed, we confess, is the mystery of our religion." The word "mystery," as used in the New Testament, refers to something which previously has not been known but now is made known. It carries also the more usual connotation of the word "mystery." The mystery of which Paul speaks is something that calls forth wonder and awe. The word translated "religion" in the Revised Standard Version is rendered "godliness" in other translations. This adds an important shade of meaning, for Paul was talking of the mystery which makes for godliness in the lives of those who receive it.

The great mystery of our religion is defined in six clauses. Most commentators feel that Paul is quoting here from an early hymn, in which the Christians bore witness to their faith. For the first statement, *"He* was manifested in the flesh," some ancient manuscripts read, *"God* was manifested in the flesh." The Revised Standard Version is probably correct, but the two expressions have the same meaning, for the pronoun "he" undoubtedly refers to Jesus. The expression, "manifested in the flesh," is reminiscent of John 1:1, 14 and Philippians 2:5-11. The Son of God entered the context of our earthly life and into the complete range of our human experiences. This is the mystery of the Incarnation, the supreme mystery of the God-man.

He who was manifested in the flesh was "vindicated in the Spirit." The Revised Standard Version makes a mistake by capitalizing the "s" in "spirit." The reference is not to the Holy Spirit but to spirit in contrast to flesh. He who was manifested in the flesh made tremendous claims for himself. He claimed to have power to forgive sins; he asserted that he was in a unique sense the Son of God. And the claims of this one individual in history who dared to say that he was God were vindicated. They were vindicated by his mighty acts and by his resurrection from the dead.

He was "seen by angels." The mighty drama of redemption which was wrought out on our earth was seen by spiritual beings other than men (compare I Peter 1:12). Christ was "preached among the nations," that is, among the Gentiles. To Paul the supreme mystery of the faith was that the redemption which had been wrought out in Jesus Christ was freely offered to the Gentiles. Here is a salvation for all mankind. He was "believed on in the world." When the first Christians gave their witness to Jesus Christ, to his life and death and resurrection, they found that their witness was believed. In response to their preaching there came into being in the great centers of the ancient world little groups of people who acknowledged Jesus to be the God-man. The final phrase is out of order in point of time. The Ascension came before the proclamation. But Paul's progression closes with the consummation of the movement, when he who was manifested in the flesh and vindicated in the spirit was received up into glory, that is, when Jesus Christ is seated at the right hand of God in glory and in power. The great mystery which is at the heart of the Christian faith is the mystery of the God-man, the mystery of the Person of Jesus Christ. It is at this point especially that Christianity is unique, different from all the other religions of the world. The whole statement is made in connection with the assertion that the Church is the pillar of the truth. If we are to know the ultimate truth about the universe we must come to know the mystery of our religion, the witness of the Church to the God-man. The Church is not the source of truth. Truth exists independently of us. Jesus is the Son of God whether we acknowledge him or not. But for a truth to have power it must be believed. The Church is the community of those who acknowledge Jesus as Lord. The Christian faith has power to change the world when it is embraced by a living community of those who believe it firmly enough to live by it or to die for it. In this sense, the Church is the pillar of the truth.

The Goodness of Creation (4:1-5)

In the opening verses of chapter 4 Timothy is warned of false teachings which he is certain to face. The appearance of false teachers has already been predicted by the Spirit in some prophetic utterance known to Paul. Furthermore, Paul may have felt that at least in germ these distorters of the gospel message were to be found among the false teachers at Ephesus. The heresy which was being communicated had two practical expressions. These teachers were forbidding marriage and were enjoining upon their followers abstinence from certain foods as a religious duty. The two ideas probably had a common root in asceticism, the doctrine that by certain types of self-denial a man can achieve a high spiritual state. The attempt was being made to give the sanction of the Christian faith to Greek and Oriental ideas which were quite foreign to the inner meaning of the gospel. In First Corinthians (chs. 6-7), Paul had dealt with the Christian understanding of marriage. There he advised against marriage in some situations as a matter of expediency, but he upheld the institution of marriage as ordained of God. And in Ephesians 5:21-33 he used the self-giving of man and woman in marriage as an illustration of the relation of Christ to his Church. Paul's teaching here supplements but does not contradict the earlier epistles. In this letter he insists that there is no peculiar holiness in refraining from marriage. The implications of this are far-reaching when we consider the way in which the vow of celibacy has been involved in monastic orders both for men and women in some branches of the Christian faith.

In the same way Paul would teach that there is no peculiar holiness in abstaining from meats. Christians need to discipline their eating in relation to health, to eat for strength and not for gluttony. When food is scarce Christians may choose to eat less in order that they may have more to share with others. But there is no religious value in hunger for its own sake. The true Christian attitude is to recognize the goodness of creation and to receive with thanksgiving the gifts of God. The attitude which is expressed here with regard to marriage and the eating of meats can be applied to other things. Christians do not need, for conscience' sake, to deny themselves the legitimate sources of pleasure. They have a right to enjoy some of the comforts and conveniences of life; they can appreciate the beauty of the world of nature; they should seek to understand art and music. The good things of life, if received with thanksgiving, are for the use of the Christian.

This does not mean, of course, that the Christian is not to know discipline. He must satisfy the desires of the body within the limits which are set for him in the word of the Lord. He must avoid drunkenness and gluttony. He must shun immorality. And as a good soldier of Jesus Christ he must be prepared at all times to endure hardness. But the desires of the body are not in themselves evil. A man does not become holy because he is hungry and thirsty, frustrated in his sex life, and uncomfortable in his living conditions. There is no religious value in irritating the skin with a hair shirt.

Paul warned Timothy against the concept of the body as evil. But he could hardly have foreseen the full extent to which Christianity was later to be distorted by this very concept, which is quite foreign to the faith that God manifests himself in the flesh. It is with a certain sense of outrage that we contemplate the extent to which, in the name of religion, Christian men and women have been denied the normal expressions of natural desires. Asceticism penetrated the Church early in her history, and not until the time of the Reformation was there a satisfactory return to the understanding of the goodness of creation and its implications for human life which Paul expresses so clearly.

Training in Godliness (4:6-10)

It is appropriate that the discussion of the goodness of creation and the rejection of asceticism should be followed by a paragraph in which Paul urges upon Timothy the inner discipline which is appropriate to the Christian life. The "instructions" of 4:6 call to mind the instructions on the way people should behave in the family of God (3:14-15). The reference is probably to the instructions of the letter as a whole, but perhaps particularly to the warning against asceticism. If Timothy heeds these instructions and teaches them to his people, he will be a good minister of Jesus Christ. As part of his training, Timothy is to resolve to have nothing to do with "godless and silly myths." These godless myths are contrasted with the central mystery of the Christian faith, which is the doctrine of the Incarnation, the witness to the God-man (see comment on 3:16). This is admittedly a great mystery, but it is a mystery which makes for godliness, for righteous living.

But it is not enough to reject silly and godless myths. Timothy must train himself in godliness. "Bodily training is of some value." We are all familiar with the training of the body which is necessary if we are to excel in sports. The Greeks especially placed a great deal of emphasis on the training of the body. More important, however, than the discipline of the body for success in sports is the consistent discipline of the body over the years in order to keep it strong and well that we may have strength for the tasks laid upon us. It is essential to observe the rhythm of rest and exercise, to eat the foods that are nourishing and to eat in moderation, to avoid habit-forming drinks or drugs, to give the body adequate medical care. The discipline of the body is necessary if we are to have the requisite physical strength for effective work.

Paul does not depreciate the importance of training the body but he does contrast it with what he calls training in godliness, referring to the spiritual discipline which is necessary if the conditions for growth in grace and in the knowledge of Jesus Christ are to be met. We can be sure that such training includes the reading of the Word of God, the reading of good books, the practice of prayer, attendance at public worship, the effort to be obedient to the Word of God, stewardship of time, money, and abilities, and the like. Training in godliness is of value because it holds promise for the present life. The deepest satisfactions in this present life come to those who give themselves to such training. A line of an old hymn declares, "Solid joys and lasting pleasure none but Zion's children know." Those who walk the way of inner spiritual discipline find the key to the best things in this present life—the deep inner satisfactions which come when life is lived out in obedience to Christ and in the service of fellow man.

Training in godliness is valuable also because it holds promise for the life to come. Christians believe that they are following a way of life which will lead in the end to laying hold on the life to come. The end of this present life is not the end of human existence. There is a life to come. Those who acknowledge Jesus as Lord and follow him are walking a road which leads to an enriched life beyond the grave. In verse 9 is inserted the statement, "The saying is sure and worthy of full acceptance." Grammatically this can apply either to verse 8 or to verse 10. But it probably refers to the statement just made. The belief that the way of the Christ is the way to eternal life is one of the great certainties of the Christian faith.

The Christian is concerned for training in godliness because he knows that this way of life holds promise for the present life and also for the life to come. But he is under no illusions. He knows that he has hope for the life to come because his hope is set on the living God. We can never find our way to the eternal home in our own strength. We must hope for the *living* God to meet us in the hour of death and take us to be with him. This living God is described as "the Savior of all men, especially of those who believe." God is the Savior of all men in the sense that his saving purpose reaches to all men (see 2:3-4). God is the Savior of all men in that the one Mediator, the man Christ Jesus, gave himself a ransom for all (2:6). But this salvation which God in Christ has wrought out for all men becomes effective for those who believe. In this sense, God is "the Savior . . . especially of those who believe."

The Discipline of the Minister (4:11-16)

The theme of the necessity for spiritual discipline is continued in verses 11-16, with special reference to the discipline of the minister. Paul may have inserted the advice, "Let no one despise your youth," in the knowledge that the letter would be read by the elders at Ephesus. At this time Timothy must have been at least forty years old, but he was young in comparison with Paul and some of the older men at Ephesus. He could avoid criticisms of his youth by bearing himself in a way that would reveal his maturity. He is to "set the believers an example in speech and conduct, in love, in faith, in purity" (vs. 12). The minister commends himself to his congregation when they see in him a model of the kind of person the Christian should be in thought and life. The minister must be a living example of the faith which he professes. In verse 13 Paul reminds Timothy again of his hope of coming to him at Ephesus (see 3:14). But in the meantime Timothy is to give attention to the public reading of Scripture, to preaching, and to teaching—the public functions of a minister of the gospel. The Greek here has simply "give attention to reading," but it is clear from the setting that the reference is to the public reading of the Scriptures and not to the minister's private habits of reading. Of course the Scriptures would be the Old Testament. But there soon developed in the churches the habit of reading in public letters of Paul and other Christian documents. This custom was to play a large part in the formation of the Canon of the New Testament.

Verse 14, like II Timothy 1:6, refers to a special gift which Timothy possessed (see also I Timothy 1:18; 5:22). It seems that this gift was predicted in prophetic utterances. It also seems that there was public recognition of it in a service which involved the laying on of hands. In this passage Paul reminds Timothy of the time when the elders laid their hands upon him. And in II Timothy 1:6, he writes: "Hence I remind you to rekindle the gift of God that is within you through the laying on of my hands." This may refer to one service in which Paul joined with the elders in the laying on of hands, or it may refer to a special service in which Paul alone participated. In either case, the reference is to a peculiar gift which Timothy had received which is not defined. The setting suggests a certain aptitude for order and administration, but this is only a possibility. The whole theory of apostolic succession can be read into the verses, but in their setting they do not demand it.

The special gift of Timothy is listed along with the accepted duties of public reading of the Scriptures, preaching, and teaching. Timothy is to give himself to these duties in such a way that all men may become aware of his improvement as he discharges the duties of the ministry. The advice is summed up in the injunction: "Take heed to yourself and to your teaching; hold to that, for by so doing you will save both yourself and your hearers" (vs. 16). The construction of the sentence is awkward, but the meaning is clarified in a paraphrase: "Take heed to yourself and your teaching; if you will do that, you will save both yourself and your hearers." This is excellent advice for the minister of a congregation. The minister must be concerned with his own spiritual discipline. In the development of the spiritual life, he cannot lead others any farther than he is willing to go himself.

He must also be concerned in his preaching and teaching to be faithful to the inner meaning of the gospel. And he must preach a message that is relevant to the lives of his people. If he will take heed to himself and his teaching, he will save himself. The reference here is not to his eternal salvation but to his work as a minister. He will save himself for the ministry of the gospel, and in so doing he will save his hearers. He will bring to his people the message which they need for their salvation in this present life "and also for the life to come" (4:8).

Respect for All Persons (5:1-2)

In these verses, Paul defines Timothy's attitude toward various age groups in the church. He is to show respect for the older men by advising or exhorting them rather than by rebuking them openly. He is to treat the younger men as brothers, the older women as mothers, and the younger women as sisters. Paul throws in a word of caution when he adds, "in all purity."

The Treatment of Widows (5:3-16)

As background for the understanding of this long passage, it is necessary to remember the dependent condition of widows in the ancient world. A woman who was left a widow had very little opportunity to enter the labor market and earn a living for herself. Underlying the whole passage there is the assumption of the responsibility of the Christian community to care for those members of its fellowship who cannot be provided for in any other way. This is the only passage in the Pastoral Epistles in which the ministry of the Church in relief work is discussed. The position taken here is very similar to that which is set forth in the Letters to the Thessalonians. Paul is deeply concerned that those who are in need shall be adequately taken care of, but he is also very anxious to preserve the independence of the family groups and to leave in the home the first responsibility for the care of dependents. "If a widow has children or grandchildren, let them first learn their religious duty to their own family and make some return to their parents; for this is acceptable in the sight of God" (vs. 4). In development of the same idea Paul writes: "If any one does not provide for his relatives, and especially for his own family, he has disowned the faith and is worse than an unbeliever" (vs. 8). If a Christian does not provide for his own family he is not living up to the teachings of his faith; he is not even living up to the universal sense of responsibility of every man to provide for his own family which is found even among those who do not embrace the Christian faith. Paul does not mean that the man who does not provide for his family is an apostate from the Christian faith. He simply means that he is not living up to his own professed creed or even to the ethical code of his pagan neighbors. Paul returns to this theme in verse 16. He has advised the younger widows if possible to marry again and establish themselves in a family situation. And then he places on women, in their responsibility for running the home, the same concern for widows that he has asked the men to assume. "If any believing woman has relatives who are widows, let her assist them; let the church not be burdened, so that it may assist those who are real widows."

The injunction given here needs to be heard in the modern world. In many situations today the Church is not carrying the major load of the care of the dependent persons of the community. This is to be accounted for in part by the way in which the state has entered the field of administering relief to those in need. But whether relief is carried on by the Church or by the state, or by Church and state working together, the basic responsibility of the family unit for the care of its dependent members needs to be emphasized again. In many cases children have a tendency to assume very little responsibility for their parents, not to mention the grandparents or the uncles and aunts. The first responsibility for the care of dependents lies with the family. This responsibility cannot be expressed in terms of financial obligations alone. It is the responsibility of the family to give to all of its members the security of knowing that they are loved and cared for. Of course this involves, on the part of each member of the family group, the readiness to carry to the limit of his ability his share of the load.

It would seem that there was in the Church at the time when Paul wrote, a loosely organized order of older widows who ministered to others in the name of Christ and his Church and who were at least in part supported by the Church. It would also seem that some of these women had not always borne themselves in such a way as to reflect credit on the Christian community. It is in this setting that Paul urges the younger widows to marry and advises Timothy against enrolling a widow who is less than sixty years old.

The Elders (5:17-25)

In these verses Timothy is given directions for his supervision of the elders of the church. He had been sent to Ephesus in order to administer discipline. The directions given here are sufficiently general to apply to the building of morale in any group of church officers. The elders who rule well should be considered worthy of "double honor." The emphasis here is on the basic responsibility of the elders for the government of the church, but special honor should be given to the elders who labor in preaching and teaching.

It is in connection with the elder who labors in preaching and teaching that Paul argues for the support of the ministry. The same thought is given in a much more expanded form in I Corinthians 9:1-18. The argument is based on a verse from Deuteronomy: "You shall not muzzle an ox when it treads out the grain" (Deut. 25:4). Of course, in its original setting the verse does not bear directly on the support of the ministry. But if one shows such concern for the ox when it is treading out the grain, he should also be concerned for the support of the elder who labors in preaching and teaching. Paul also quotes the statement, "The laborer deserves his wages." This is found among the sayings of Jesus in Luke 10:7. Paul probably refers to it in I Corinthians 9:14.

Verse 19 deals with the central problem of maintaining the character of the elders in order that the governing body of the church may hold the respect and confidence of the membership. Charges against those who have been made elders are not to be received lightly. An accusation against an elder should not be considered unless it can be supported by two or three witnesses. But if an elder persists in sin and the charges against him are sustained, it is Timothy's responsibility to rebuke him in the presence of the other elders, in order that they may be warned against this type of misconduct. Verse 21 is a charge to Timothy in his capacity as a judge, when charges have been made and an elder is being tried before him. He is to act as one who stands in the presence of God and of Christ Jesus and the elect angels. The reference is to the final judgment scene, when Christ returns with his angels to judge the world. The phrase "elect angels" is better rendered "chosen angels." They are the angels whom Christ has chosen to bring with him on the Day of Judgment (see II Thess. 1:7). The passage as a whole shows the serious necessity of administering discipline in the governing body of the church.

Paul's concern for the integrity and strength of the elders leads him to write: "Do not be hasty in the laying on of hands, nor participate in another man's sins; keep yourself pure" (vs. 22). The first part of the verse is a needed warning against undue haste in ordaining men as elders. In 3:6, Paul advised against ordaining as elders men who are recent converts, feeling that a man should be tested before he is trusted with the responsibilities of the elder. At first thought there seems to be little connection between the warning against being hasty in the laying on of hands and the words, "Nor participate in another man's sins." But if a minister ordains a man as an elder and works with him in the church, he becomes in a sense responsible for the character of the man he has put forward in this way. And if the man is known to be subject to serious criticism in his moral and spiritual life, the minister compromises himself by continuing to support him in his office as elder.

It is in connection with this danger that Paul writes to Timothy: "Keep yourself pure." The minister must be very careful not to be compromised in his stand for righteousness by endorsing men who are not worthy of his trust. Having said this, Paul in typical fashion goes off at a tangent from his use of the word "pure." He remembers that Timothy, in his effort to keep himself free from all criticism, has taken his stand as a "water drinker." The reference is, of course, to the use of wine. Timothy is numbered among those who practice total abstinence. But Paul knows that Timothy has "frequent ailments." (We would judge from this that Timothy, although only about forty years old, was not in vigorous health.) Hence the discourse on discipline is interrupted as Paul advises Timothy to take a little wine for his stomach's sake (vs. 23). This verse has been quoted many times because it seems to lend Paul's support to the use of wine in moderation rather than to the position of total abstinence. However, it should be remembered that Paul gives this advice to a man who is known as a total abstainer. And we should notice that he says "a little wine" and "for the sake of your stomach," that is, for medicinal purposes. We cannot be sure that Paul's medical advice carries with it his authority as an Apostle. But we can be reasonably sure that any medical value found in alcoholic beverages can be found also in present-day medicines which are not habit-forming. In the light of the whole situation which faces the Church in the handling of alcohol today, a strong case can be made for total abstinence in terms of avoiding a habit-forming stimulant and in terms of the Christian's influence on others. Paul's advice to Timothy does nothing to undermine this argument (see Rom. 14:21).

Verse 24 returns to the theme of warning against undue haste in the making of elders. The sins of some men are so obvious to the whole community that no one would think of electing them to the office of elder. One thinks, for example, of men who are known for their drunkenness, their profanity, or their immorality. But the sins of other men are not so obvious. It is only as we know them well that we can realize the extent to which they are not qualified for the responsibility of serving as elders of the church. The same thing is true of the good deeds of life. In some cases good deeds are conspicuous; others are done quietly, without notice, but in time they will not remain hidden, and when they do come out they will reveal the real character of those who have performed them.

A Message to Slaves (6:1-2)

This is the first reference to slavery in the Pastoral Epistles. It comes up again in Titus 2:9-10 and will receive more extended treatment in the comment on the Letter to Philemon. Earlier Paul dealt with this matter in Ephesians 6:5-9 and Colossians 3:22-25. Galatians 3:28 and Colossians 3:11 show how the division between master and slave is transcended in Christ. (Peter deals with slavery in I Peter 2:18-20.) The present passage fits into the pattern of the treatment of slavery in other New Testament passages. The institution of slavery is accepted as part of the form of the economic order. No direct attempt is made to call in question the premises upon which the institution is founded. The informed Christian conscience, however, came to see the violation of human personality involved in the ownership of one man by another. The writers of the New Testament do bring to bear on masters and slaves the implications of the Christian ethic within the institution of slavery. In this passage Paul speaks to slaves only, urging them to show respect to their masters "that the name of God and the teaching may not be defamed." Verse 2 deals with the special case of Christian slaves

who have Christian masters. Paul assumes that within the
church fellowship, masters and slaves meet as brothers. He is
anxious that slaves should not take advantage of this situation
but should look upon their masters as "believers and beloved."
Within the fellowship of the Church the relationship of masters
and slaves was being transformed by the implications of the
Christian faith.

The Perils of Riches (6:3-10)

Verse 3 returns to the initial theme of the letter—directions to
Timothy concerning the handling of false teachers at Ephesus.
The principle is set forth that all Christian teaching is to be judged
by its agreement with "the sound words of our Lord Jesus Christ
and the teaching which accords with godliness," that is, the teaching which makes for righteous living. The two ideas are not placed
in opposition to each other. If teaching is in agreement with
the sound words of Jesus Christ it will make for godly living.
The phrase, "the sound words of our Lord Jesus Christ," obviously refers to the teaching which the Church has received
from her Lord. When Paul wrote, some of the Church's memory
of the teachings of Jesus may have been still preserved in oral
form although much of it had undoubtedly been committed to
writing. In his teachings concerning the stewardship of possessions, which is the central theme of the passage, Paul consistently
reflects the teachings of Jesus on this subject. Verses 4-5 give a
somewhat uncomplimentary description of the teachers at Ephesus (and at other places) who do not agree with "the sound
words of our Lord Jesus Christ." They imagine that "godliness
is a means of gain." This is the starting point for a discussion of
the spiritual perils involved in the desire to be rich. The meaning
of the gospel is distorted when godliness is considered to be a
way of gain. Paul has defended the right of the elder who labors
in preaching and teaching to receive some compensation for his
labors (5:17-18), but Christian teachers must never think of
their ministry as a means of making money.

In verse 6 Paul takes his cue from the word "gain," and adds
that godliness with contentment is great gain. He then defines
the limits within which material goods can serve men as he reminds us that we brought nothing into this world and can take
nothing out. In the total span of human existence, as seen in
the Christian faith, the period of life in this world is short, but

it is only within this brief period that material possessions can serve. We are, therefore, to be content with the simple necessities of food and clothing. The need for shelter and other things which are necessary for decent living would, of course, be included in these limits.

Against the background of this statement, Paul points out the spiritual dangers involved in the restless desire to be rich. Men are in spiritual peril when the desire to grow rich in material possessions becomes the consuming passion of their lives. It is in this setting that the familiar saying comes, "The love of money is the root of all evils." A more exact statement of the truth which Paul is setting forth appears in the translation, "The love of money is a root of all kinds of evil." The love of money is not *the* root of all evil. Evil roots in the rebellious wills of men; in the uncontrolled lusts of men. It roots in man's refusal to find the center of his being in obedience to the will of his Creator. But the love of money can become a root of almost every kind of evil. The love of money is a major root of most of our social evils. "It is through this craving that some have wandered away from the faith and pierced their hearts with many pangs" (vs. 10).

The Good Fight of Faith (6:11-16)

The man of God should shun the dangers involved in false attitudes toward money and should aim, instead, at "righteousness, godliness, faith, love, steadfastness, gentleness." He is to "fight the good fight of the faith." When, in II Timothy 4:7, Paul says, "I have fought the good fight," he means that he has identified himself with the battle for righteousness and has given himself as a good soldier in the cause of Jesus Christ. He probably has very much the same meaning in this charge to Timothy. Timothy is not to be controlled by the desire to be rich. Instead he is to give himself without reserve in the cause of Jesus Christ. In so doing, he is to take hold of the eternal life to which he was called when he "made the good confession in the presence of many witnesses," clearly a reference to his baptism. It was at that time that Timothy made his public confession of faith in Jesus Christ as Lord and Savior and gave his response to the call to eternal life. If we acknowledge Jesus before men, we have his promise that he will acknowledge us before his Father in heaven (Matt. 10:32).

Verse 13 prepares for a charge to Timothy. The reference to God as the one "who gives life to all things" is probably spoken against the background of Timothy's taking hold of the eternal life. Similarly, the time when Timothy "made the good confession" in the presence of many witnesses suggests the fact that Christ Jesus "in his testimony before Pontius Pilate made the good confession." Pilate was the Roman governor of Judea in A.D. 30. The Apostles' Creed touches history at this point in the phrase "suffered under Pontius Pilate." For Timothy the good confession was his acknowledgment of Jesus as Lord. What was the good confession which Jesus made in his testimony before Pontius Pilate? It would be his claim to be the Christ, the Son of God. In both cases the good confession is the witness as to *who Jesus is*.

The charge which Paul makes to Timothy is to "keep the commandment unstained and free from reproach until the appearing of our Lord Jesus Christ" (vs. 14). The commandment is not defined, but it probably refers to the commands which Jesus has given to his Church. If this interpretation is correct we have here an anticipation of verse 20, in which Timothy is told to guard the deposit. The commandments of the Lord are to be remembered in his Church until he returns. They are not to be distorted or adulterated with the commandments of men. Paul expresses the hope of the return of Christ which held so dominant a place in his thinking in Thessalonians. He does not attempt to date it but says that God will manifest it "at the proper time." The reference to the appearing of our Lord Jesus Christ is followed by a great doxology to God the Father (vss. 15-16).

A Charge to the Rich (6:17-19)

Verse 11 opened with the phrase, "But as for you, man of God," and in verses 13-14 a charge was given to Timothy as a man of God. The charge described the central purpose of his life, in contrast to the controlling purpose of those who desire to be rich. It is appropriate therefore that Paul should give now a charge to those to whom God has given riches in this world. The charge is so simple that it does not need extended comment, but it is so far-reaching that its observance by the rich would have a profound influence on our civilization. The rich are not to be haughty or to set their hope on uncertain riches but on God, "who richly furnishes us with everything to enjoy." They are to do good and to be rich in good deeds. Thus they are to lay up for themselves treasures in heaven, so that they, with Timothy, may take hold of the life that is life indeed.

The Deposit of Faith (6:20-21)

The idea expressed here becomes more central in Second Timothy, when Paul knows that his earthly pilgrimage is about to end. That which "has been entrusted" to Timothy is the deposit of faith, the truth which has been revealed through Jesus Christ and committed to the keeping of mortal men. Faith is, of course, first of all personal commitment to Jesus Christ as Lord and Savior. In the Christian faith we are dealing with a person rather than with an idea. But in the revelation of God in Christ there is involved a body of convictions concerning God, man, and the universe which Christians must continue to embrace in the midst of the changing circumstances of earthly existence. The message of the gospel has been committed to Timothy. He is to preserve it in its purity and proclaim it in its power.

THE GOSPEL OF GOD
II Timothy 1:1-18

Greetings (1:1-2)

Nothing is known about the background of Second Timothy apart from the information which can be gathered from the letter itself. The letter is deeply personal and revealing. When First Timothy was written, Paul was a free man. He had sent Timothy to Ephesus and hoped soon to join him there. The Letter to Titus was also written while Paul was free to carry on active missionary work. But Second Timothy was written from prison in Rome. Moreover, it reflects a very different attitude from that of the letters of the first imprisonment, such as Colossians. During the first imprisonment Paul was awaiting trial as an uncondemned man who expected to be released. By the time of the second imprisonment the whole attitude of the Roman state toward Christianity had changed. In this letter, Paul is a condemned man, the leader of a persecuted sect; he has had a preliminary trial and now has no expectation of avoiding the death sentence. It is dangerous for his friends to come to him. For one reason or another all but Luke have left him. Onesiphorus has had difficulty in finding him. In this setting, Paul writes a letter which is his last word to Timothy and also the last word of the great Apostle to the Church he has served. In the letter he seeks to nerve Timothy for the time of persecution. In so doing, he paints for all time a picture of the faithful Christian minister. In this intimate message to his beloved son in the faith, Paul reveals his own deep emotions as he stands at the end of the road, looking back on his life as an Apostle of Christ and forward to the life with Christ which lies beyond the grave.

The greetings of the letter follow the pattern of the First Letter to Timothy. Again Paul affirms his apostleship. He is a man who has been sent by Jesus Christ. He has become an Apostle not of his own choice but by the will of God. And the central purpose of his ministry has been to declare "the promise of the life which is in Christ Jesus." He writes to Timothy as to a beloved child. In the earlier letter, the emphasis has been on the way in which Timothy is his true spiritual son in the faith; here the emphasis is on the depth of his love for Timothy. The latter part of verse 2 is identical in the two epistles.

A Prayer of Thanksgiving for Timothy (1:3-7)

In First Timothy, Paul has described himself as the "foremost of sinners" (1:15). Here he says that he serves God with "a clear conscience." In the first instance, Paul was thinking of his activity as the persecutor of the Christian Church; here he is looking back on the years in which he has not been disobedient to the heavenly vision (see also Acts 24:15-16).

Verse 3 also expresses Paul's sense of the continuity of his faith with that of his fathers. To him, Christianity was the true development of Judaism.

The depth of love between the two men is indicated by the moving words of verse 4. Verse 5 is one of the most familiar verses of the letter, a favorite of those who wish to emphasize the importance of family religion. It suggests the way in which the faith of the parents becomes alive in the hearts of their children. As a background for emphasis on family religion the verse is supplemented by II Timothy 3:14-15, which describes the training in the Scriptures which Timothy received in his home.

The gift which is referred to in verse 6 appears also in I Timothy 4:14 (see the comment there). The gift is not clearly defined here, but verse 7 seems to refer to it: "God did not give us a spirit of timidity but a spirit of power and love and self-control." At their ordination Paul and Timothy received that divine sustaining of the human spirit which makes for power and for love and for self-control.

Timothy's Witness to Jesus Christ (1:8-10)

Because Timothy has received the spirit of power, he is to be bold in his proclamation of the gospel. He is not to be ashamed of giving his testimony to Jesus Christ, and he is not to be ashamed of Paul because he is a prisoner. This is our first indication of Paul's situation. Paul is suffering for his faith, and Timothy must be ready to take his share of suffering for the gospel also.

The reference to the gospel and the power of God leads to a brief summary of the gospel. God has "saved us and called us with a holy calling, not in virtue of our works but in virtue of his own purpose and the grace which he gave us in Christ Jesus ages ago." In this great Pauline statement the ultimate basis of

salvation is seen to rest in the purpose of God to redeem a
people for himself through the redemptive work of Christ. Attention needs to be focused on this statement, since the major emphasis of the Pastoral Epistles is upon the importance of good
works. But this statement, alongside Titus 3:5, indicates that
all dependence upon good works as the basis of our hope of
salvation is rejected, and there stands out the great Pauline position of salvation by faith alone, through grace alone, to the glory
of God alone. The ultimate mystery of redemption must always
be left in the mystery of the divine will, a will that is free but
not irresponsible.

The gospel roots in the divine decision to save men through
Jesus Christ. This eternal, redemptive purpose of God was not
fully manifested to us until the time of the appearance of our
Savior Christ Jesus. The work of Jesus is summarized in the
statement that he "abolished death and brought life and immortality to light through the gospel." Of course Jesus did not abolish
physical death. Both before and after the coming of Jesus all
of our human life is marked by existence unto death. But Jesus
conquered death. He died and rose again on the third day. He
gives his witness to the resurrection life of God which lies beyond
death. He tells his followers that he has gone to prepare a place
for them and that he will come again and receive them unto
himself, that where he is they may be also (John 14:3). He
abolishes the fear of death for his followers and gives to them
an assured hope of entrance into the heavenly home. In so doing,
he brings to light "life and immortality" through the gospel.
Through the work of Jesus, the hope of immortality is brought
into the light of the divine revelation. Thus, in the message of
the gospel men are called to become partakers of an eternal
salvation.

Paul's Witness to Jesus Christ (1:11-14)

In the foregoing summary of the gospel, Paul speaks in im-
personal terms. But in verse 11 he gives his personal relation to
this message of redemption which has been manifested in the
appearance of Jesus Christ. He has been appointed a preacher,
an apostle, and a teacher of this gospel. To him there has been
committed the proclamation of the good news of what God has
done in Christ. It is because Paul has been faithful in delivering
the message which has been committed unto him that he is now

in prison. We are reminded of his statement to King Agrippa, "I stand here on trial for hope in the promise made by God to our fathers," and his question: "Why is it thought incredible by any of you that God raises the dead?" (Acts 26:4-8).

Paul is in a Roman prison and knows that for him the end is not far away, but he has no apologies to make for his life and no fears as he faces the future. He is "not ashamed" because he is certain that he has put his confidence in the right Person. He has ventured all for Jesus Christ, and he is sure that he has not made a mistake. He knows the One in whom he has believed. Paul's knowledge of Jesus would include, of course, his knowledge of the testimony to Jesus which he received from those who had known him in the flesh. It would include also his memory of the time when the Risen Lord confronted him on the road to Damascus and called him to become the Apostle to the Gentiles. But it would include, in addition, the knowledge of Jesus which had come to him in a long life of obedience to his Lord. In his communion with the living Lord there were for Paul mystical experiences which are not given to most of us. Against the background of the total experiences of his life Paul can say, "I know whom I have believed."

Because he has complete confidence in Christ Jesus, Paul can write: "I am sure that he is able to guard until that Day what has been entrusted to me." The expression "until that Day" refers to the return of Christ, the consummation of history in the coming of the Kingdom of God. A disputed point in the interpretation of verse 12 is in the question of what it is that the Christ is to guard. The margin of the Revised Standard Version gives as an alternate translation for the close of the verse the clause, "what I have entrusted to him." The Greek has simply the words "my deposit," hence either translation is possible. In one case the reference would be to the hope of an eternal salvation which Paul has committed to Jesus Christ. This fits in with his description of the Christ as the one who has abolished death and brought immortality to light. And of course such an expression of the hope of an eternal salvation is true to the message of the gospel, regardless of whether or not it is set forth in this text. But it is equally proper to say that what Paul is concerned about here is the fate of the gospel in the world. Since Paul knows that his end is near, he is concerned about the preservation of the purity of the message of the gospel. But he is confident that the living Lord will be able to guard to the end of earthly history the integrity of the message which Paul has been preaching. This interpretation fits in with the thought which follows, where Paul urges Timothy to be faithful to the message which he has received and to guard it as the truth which has been entrusted to him by the Holy Spirit. It is in the power of the indwelling Spirit that Timothy is to proclaim the truth of the gospel to his generation.

A Tribute to Onesiphorus (1:15-18)

The charge to Timothy is interrupted by two personal reminiscences. The first of these is an unpleasant memory, the second a rich tribute to an otherwise unknown man. Timothy has heard of the way in which some Christians who are now in Asia turned away from Paul. The reference is probably to the failure of these men to stand by him in his time of trial. This is one of many indications this letter gives of the tense situation in Rome, where it is now dangerous for men to identify themselves with Paul and his work. Paul names two of the men who have deserted him. The specific mention of Phygelus and Hermogenes may be due to Paul's knowledge of their presence in Ephesus.

Against the background of the failure of these men, the fidelity of Onesiphorus can be appreciated. He and his family lived at Ephesus. His record of service in the church there was well known to Timothy. For some reason Onesiphorus had to come to Rome, where he had searched among the prisoners until he found Paul. This may not have been easy, because at this time Paul was probably closely guarded. But Onesiphorus found him and visited him on several occasions. He seems to have ignored the element of risk involved in identifying himself with the condemned leader of a proscribed sect. His visits were helpful to Paul, bringing refreshment to the lonely prisoner and strengthening the spirit of the great Apostle. Paul prays that the Lord will grant mercy to the family of Onesiphorus and that this friend will find mercy from the Lord at the Day of Judgment. At the close of the letter Paul sends greetings to this family (4:19). Some commentators think that these passages suggest that Onesiphorus is dead at the time of the writing of this epistle. In this case, Paul would be praying for a man who is dead. A more likely assumption is that Onesiphorus was at the time away from his family in Ephesus.

THE FAITHFUL CHRISTIAN PASTOR

II Timothy 2:1-26

A Disciplined Minister of the Gospel (2:1-7)

Against the background of the desertion by those of Asia and
the loyalty of Onesiphorus, Paul urges Timothy to be strengthened in the virtues and spiritual powers which are available in
Christ Jesus. In verse 2 he returns to his concern for the transmission of the faith in its purity. Paul is speaking, of course, of
the content of the gospel message. Timothy has received this
from Paul and also from other witnesses. (The reference may be
to those from whom Paul has received much of his information.)
In turn Timothy is to transmit the faith he has received. It is to
be the *same* faith, not a modified version of it. He is to transmit
it to men who are known to be sound in the faith and also known
to have the capacity to teach others. When Paul wrote, he had
to depend on Timothy and those taught by Timothy for the
transmission to the next generation of a sound understanding
of the Christian faith. Of course, in addition, the greatest letters
of Paul were already written, and the witness of the Church to
her Lord, which has been preserved in the Gospels, was in the
process of being collected and written down. Thus, in time, there
would come into being a written Word which would become
both the norm and the source of Christian preaching and
teaching.

An urgent theme to Paul is his concern that Timothy, his son
in the faith, shall be adequate for his tasks as a Christian minister and faithful in the day of persecution. It is with this concern
in mind that Paul urges Timothy to take his share of suffering
"as a good soldier of Christ Jesus." Paul has no patience with
asceticism or self-inflicted punishments as a form of spiritual
penance, but he is profoundly concerned that the Christian minister should be prepared to endure hardness as a disciplined soldier of Christ Jesus. He amplifies this thought with three illus-
trations. The first is suggested by the thought of the soldier. A
good soldier cannot become absorbed in civilian pursuits. He
must be free to obey the commands of the one who has en-
listed him. The Christian soldier must not become so absorbed
in the affairs of this life that he is not free to be obedient to

Jesus as Lord. The second illustration refers to the discipline of the athlete. No one goes to the top in athletics without discipline and training. The Christian minister who is to be adequate to his responsibilities must learn to discipline himself. The third illustration is that of the hard-working farmer who knows the labor which is necessary for the abundant harvest. Thus, the discipline of the minister may be expressed in his readiness to endure physical hardship in his proclamation of the gospel. It is expressed also in the mental and spiritual discipline which is a vital part of a minister's life. At times it may have to be expressed in the readiness of the minister to face unpopularity and even persecution in his fidelity to his Lord.

Faithful Unto Death (2:8-13)

Paul's summary of his entire message in the opening verses of the Letter to the Romans (Rom. 1:3-4) is helpful for an understanding of II Timothy 2:8. Through the Resurrection, Jesus is proclaimed to be the Son of God with power. In Christ's descent from David according to the flesh, there is the sign of his being fully man as well as fully God. Paul's gospel is the witness to the God-man. In fact, it is because of his witness to Jesus Christ as the God-man, with all the implications of this truth for human life, that Paul is now in prison. All the references of this letter to Paul's treatment in prison indicate that in this imprisonment he is being treated like a dangerous criminal. He writes as a prisoner wearing fetters but not as a broken man. He knows that the word of God is not bound. A faith is not necessarily destroyed when its leaders are cast into prison. Great ideas cannot be bound with fetters. The gospel which Paul had proclaimed so faithfully was being preached by others, and through this letter out of the Roman prison Paul himself was still giving his witness to Jesus Christ.

Paul accepts this difficult experience as part of the course which Jesus Christ has set for him. And he is deeply concerned that he should not falter in his final testing. He is enduring "everything for the sake of the elect, that they also may obtain the salvation which in Christ Jesus goes with eternal glory." The term "the elect" is better rendered as "the chosen." If Paul is faithful to the end, those who follow after him will be sustained by his example. And who can measure the harm that would have been done to the Christian cause if the great Apostle to the Gentiles had denied his Lord in the day of persecution?

Paul's understanding of the significance of his own suffering prepares the way for the quotation of what must have been a portion of a hymn sung by the early Christians as they faced martyrdom. It is a saying that is worthy of our complete confidence that

> If we have died with him, we shall also live with him;
> if we endure, we shall also reign with him;
> if we deny him, he also will deny us;
> if we are faithless, he remains faithful—
> for he cannot deny himself.

The first line expresses the confidence that those who die for Christ will also live with him. It was in this confidence that the early Christians faced death unafraid. The second is a call to the difficult task of enduring to the end. The tenses of the verbs here are interesting. Behind the phrase "if we have died" there is the Greek tense which expresses a single act. Behind the words "if we endure" there is a tense which expresses continual action. It is sometimes easier to die once for Christ than it is to live continually for him in the midst of constant persecution. The early Christians were confident that those who endured to the end with Christ would also reign with him. The tense of the third verb is future. It should be translated "if we shall deny him." It seems to suggest that denial of Christ by his followers is not very probable. The third line does give a solemn warning, but it is no more solemn than the warning of Jesus in Matthew 10:33. If we deny Jesus before men we may face his denial of us before his Father in heaven. If we urge men to be faithful and promise eternal life to those who endure to the end we cannot avoid asking what happens to those who do not endure to the end. The third line contains a solemn and needed warning, but the fourth line gives a message of hope.

It is possible, of course, to interpret the fourth line as confirming in even darker lines the warning of the third. There is a sense in which Christ must be faithful in the administration of punishment. But the great theme of Scripture is the faithfulness of God in spite of the fáithlessness of men. We can be confident that not every wavering of faith on our part will call down on us the awful judgment of denial by our Lord. Remember here the word of Paul to the Thessalonians: "But the Lord is faithful; he will strengthen you and guard you from evil" (II Thess. 3:3). If we put our confidence in Christ, we can face the day of testing unafraid. When we remember that Paul is thinking of Jesus who in the days of his flesh revealed his compassion and his love, we can know that the reference to his faithfulness is an expression of hope.

An Approved Workman (2:14-26)

The verses which follow are written against the background of the day of testing through persecution. In the time of trial Christians will reveal their true allegience. They will reveal it in patient endurance under persecution and, if necessary, in fidelity unto death. But it is important also to be able to distinguish between the true and false ministers of Christ in the regular routine of the ongoing work of the Church. This is particularly true when there appear teachers who distort the meaning of the gospel and misunderstand its implications for life. For this reason, Timothy is to remind the teachers at Ephesus of the need for endurance and fidelity and to charge them before the Lord to avoid wasting their time and disturbing the Church with endless and needless disputes which do not edify. The Christian teacher must always stand firm for the truth of the gospel, but he must not become involved in disputes about issues which have no practical bearing on Christian thought and life. Timothy is to do his best to present himself to God as an approved workman "who has no need to be ashamed, rightly handling the word of truth." The "word of truth" refers to the message of the gospel. The teacher who handles aright the word of truth is the person who sees the full significance of what God has said to man in Jesus Christ and understands the relevance of the gospel in the crucial issues of life. The "word of truth" is not the written Word but the Christ event, to which the written Word points. But since the knowledge of Jesus Christ comes to us through the written Word, it is also necessary for us to give ourselves to the serious study of the Bible if we are to have a true understanding of the meaning of the gospel for the world. The meaning of verse 15 is not distorted when we say that in it Paul urges us to give ourselves to hard study of Scripture. The Christian worker, moreover, is to bear himself in such a way that God can approve his handling of the Word of truth. It is this divine approval which should concern us. It will deliver us from being too deeply concerned to interpret Scripture in a manner that will win the approval of men.

Verses 16-18 give some additional comments on the false teachers, whose teaching does not lead to godliness or righteous living. Such false teaching spreads in a church as a sore spreads and destroys sound tissues of the body. Two of the false teachers are Hymenaeus and Philetus. It is probable that Hymenaeus is to be identified with the man mentioned in I Timothy 1:20, along with a man named Alexander, as having lost a good conscience and made shipwreck of his faith. Information is not available to define the exact nature of the heresy of these men. The reference seems to be to the resurrection of the Christian rather than to the resurrection of Christ. The Christian doctrine of the resurrection of the body was offensive to many of the Greeks, whc preferred to think only in terms of the immortality of the soul. The error of Hymenaeus and Philetus may have been a heresy in which the Christian hope of the resurrection of the body was explained away. Whatever the heresy was, it had resulted in upsetting the faith of some who had been members of the Christian community at Ephesus.

It is concerning those who have had their faith disturbed by the false teaching of men like Hymenaeus and Philetus that Paul writes: "God's firm foundation stands, bearing this seal: 'The Lord knows those who are his,' and, 'Let every one who names the name of the Lord depart from iniquity.' " As an old man who knows he has only a short time to live, Paul is concerned for the future of the Church in the world. But he is confident that the Church will abide, even if distressed by heresies, because God has placed her on a firm foundation. The two statements here could appropriately be inscribed on the cornerstones of church sanctuaries. The first seal of the church is contained in the words, "The Lord knows those who are his." These words may be a quotation from the words of Moses at the time of Korah's rebellion (Num. 16:5). Korah and those associated with him undertook to challenge the claim of Moses to be the man whom God had sent to lead his people. In the face of this challenge, Moses said that the Lord himself would show who was his. In the events that followed, the leadership of Moses was vindicated. But we do not have to refer to Korah's rebellion to understand the simple principle that the Lord knows those who are his. The Lord Jesus Christ looks upon all those who preach and teach in his name. He knows the difference between the true servant and the false. He knows those upon whom he can depend. Each Christian worker, as he reads these words, should be concerned for his standing with the Lord himself. He may properly ask if there is some error in his understanding of the gospel or some flaw in his character which makes it impossible for the Lord to use him effectively in his work. The permanence of the Church through the ages is based on the Lord's ability to call men to himself, even as he called Paul, and to send them out in his service.

The second seal is contained in the words, "Let every one who names the name of the Lord depart from iniquity." The first mark of the approved workman is purity of doctrine, the handling aright of the word of truth; the second mark is purity of life. The Lord's servant must apply the gospel to his own life before he can proclaim it to others. Soundness of doctrine is important, but it must always be accompanied by separation from iniquity. Remember here that Hymenaeus lost a good conscience before he made shipwreck of his faith (I Tim. 1:19-20).

Verses 20-26 continue the distinction between the approved servant and the servant who is not accepted by his Lord. The vessels which are to be found in a large home are used as illustration. Some of them will be made of gold and silver, others of wood and clay. Some will be designed for noble purposes, others will be used to hold garbage and filth. The definition of what is meant by "what is ignoble" appears in the advice to "shun youthful passions." Certainly in these youthful passions would be included such things as perversion of the sex life, failure to control thirst for alcoholic beverages, overindulgence in eating, gambling, profanity, and absorption in the pleasures of this world. Instead of giving himself to these and other youthful passions, Timothy is to "aim at righteousness, faith, love, and peace, along with those who call upon the Lord from a pure heart." The "pure heart" refers to the undivided loyalty which the Lord requires of those who would follow him. Purity of life is the second great qualification of the approved servant of the Lord.

Verse 23 repeats the warning to Timothy against becoming involved in stupid and senseless controversies which breed quarrels. This injunction is followed by a positive description of the Lord's servant. Rather than "quarrelsome," the Lord's servant must be "kindly to every one, an apt teacher, forbearing, correcting his opponents with gentleness." The bitterness with which ecclesiastical debate is sometimes carried on is a reminder that this advice is not always heeded. The Lord's servant must not compromise with heresy but must always seek to lead his opponent to repentance and the knowledge of the truth. False teachers, such as Hymenaeus and Philetus, have fallen into a snare of the Devil and have been captured by him to do his will. The teacher of false doctrine may be very useful to the Evil One. But Paul still hopes that these men may escape from the snare of the Devil and may become workmen approved of God. In these verses as a whole, he adds gentleness of spirit to soundness of doctrine and purity of life as the distinguishing marks of the true servant of the Lord.

A CHARGE TO TIMOTHY

II Timothy 3:1-17

False Teachers (3:1-9)

In the beginning of his ministry Paul expected the return of Christ in the near future. His expectation of the coming of the Lord is clearly present also in the Pastoral Epistles, but it does not dominate the scene as in the Letters to the Thessalonians. This is to be expected, for Paul, particularly in Second Timothy, writes as one who does not have long to live. As he pictures the days preceding the coming of the Lord he looks forward to an intensification of the struggle with evil and to a fuller revelation of the depths of iniquity of which human nature is capable. He has been concerned with false teachers (ch. 2), and here he sees the tendencies, already present in germ in the appearance of the false teachers at Ephesus, reaching the full dimensions of evil before the return of Christ. Against this background, he gives a summary of the vices which will appear in the lives of men as the end of the age draws near. (Compare the description of the heathen world in Romans 1:18-32.) Paul has no illusions about human nature. He is not an idealist, ignoring the depths to which the human soul can sink. Although in the present time we may have confidence in the common decency of most men, some of the things which have happened in recent years have revealed again the depths of degradation to which the human spirit can sink. Verses 2-4 seem to describe a condition into which society as a whole has degenerated; the verses which follow provide a description of the corruptions which are possible for those who have the form of religion without its power. Such corruptions have been experienced at various stages in the history of the Church. The reference to women in verse 6 is not to be taken as characteristic of the sex as a whole but of some women known to Paul who were easily led astray by false teachings. Jannes and Jambres, Egyptian magicians who opposed Moses, are not named in Exodus, but the names are given in some Jewish traditions. The folly of the false teachers will become evident in time, even as the tricks of the Egyptian magicians proved futile when they were confronted by Moses as the messenger approved of God.

Paul's Example (3:10-13)

Thinking of the contrast between the false teachers and those who are approved of God, Paul turns naturally to his own record as furnishing an example for Timothy. The themes which run through the whole of the third chapter (and, for that matter, through the letter as a whole) are the warning against false teachers, Paul's personal experiences as the basis of his testimony to the Christ and as an example of fidelity for Timothy to imitate, and his concern that Timothy prove adequate for the times of testing which are sure to come.

Verses 10-11 sum up various aspects of Paul's life which Timothy has observed. The teachings of Paul and the other Apostles provide the norm for Christian teaching in all ages. Timothy is to imitate Paul's conduct even as Paul has imitated Christ (I Cor. 11:1). A good statement of Paul's aim in life appears in II Corinthians 5:9: "We make it our aim to please him [Christ]." The faith which he proclaimed is summarized in Romans 10:9-13. His portrait of Christian love is painted in I Corinthians 13. His fidelity to his calling is shown in the way in which he was not disobedient to the heavenly vision (Acts 26:19-20).

The reference to his persecutions brings to mind the experiences of the first missionary journey. These are mentioned, not as any more severe than other experiences, but as those most closely associated with Timothy's early memories. Paul found Timothy at Lystra, and it was here that Paul had been stoned and left for dead (Acts 14:19). A much more complete account of the hardships which Paul faced is found in II Corinthians 11:21-33.

As Paul looks back on the many perils he has faced, he writes: "yet from them all the Lord rescued me." At times the rescue may have come in miraculous form, as at Philippi (Acts 16: 25-26), but at the same time the Lord called him to suffer many things for his sake (Acts 9:16), and Paul never knew complete immunity from tribulations. What he did know was that the servant of the Lord will be delivered from evil men until his work is done.

Against the background of his own persecutions, Paul writes: "Indeed all who desire to live a godly life in Christ Jesus will be persecuted." Christians do not seek persecution, and should be grateful if they are granted freedom from it. But if we follow Jesus Christ far enough we are certain to find ourselves deeply in conflict with the unchristian elements of secular society and, all too often, with the powers that be in the visible Church. The world still has effective ways of persecuting those who call in question the established mores of society. If our Christian faith has never led us into serious conflict with the evil of our world, we should begin to wonder if we have purchased immunity at the price of compromise with evil. Remember here the words of Jesus in Matthew 5:11-12. The church which does not know the meaning of persecution is apt to be a church which is not in deep tension with the injustices of modern society. As the followers of Jesus enter into a fuller understanding of the meaning of the gospel and into increasing conflict with the established customs of their society, there is a corresponding process in which those who have rejected the gospel become increasingly blind to the moral and spiritual implications of their conduct and make inevitable the struggle between those "who desire to live a godly life in Christ Jesus" and those who have rejected him.

Fidelity to the Insights of Scripture (3:14-17)

As Paul envisions the coming struggle between the followers of Jesus and false leaders, both within and outside the Church, he urges Timothy to continue in what he has learned and has firmly believed. The reference to the knowledge of the Scriptures which Timothy received as a child is to his mother, Eunice, and his grandmother, Lois, but it is proper to think that Paul includes himself as one of those from whom Timothy has learned.

In fact, Paul was Timothy's great teacher, the one who opened up to him the full meaning of the gospel of Jesus Christ. But Paul built on the foundation of the knowledge of the holy Writings which Timothy had received in his home. This reference to the Scriptures gives Paul an opportunity to set forth briefly for Timothy his understanding of the significance of the written Word. The reference, of course, is to the Old Testament. But teachings concerning the inspiration of the Old Testament which are set forth in the New Testament will naturally be applied by Christians to the inspiration of the New Testament. (See also II Peter 1:20-21 for a New Testament teaching concerning the inspiration of the Old Testament.)

Scriptures are able to make one wise unto salvation. This gives the central thrust of Scripture. The Scriptures are written to give us the knowledge which we need if we are to find salvation from sin and the power to lay hold on the way that leads to the heavenly home. The Scriptures instruct us for salvation "through faith in Christ Jesus." There are two ideas here. The first is that the Scriptures point us, not to faith in a Book, but to faith in the Person to whom the Book points. We are saved through faith in Christ Jesus. The second is that it is through faith in Christ Jesus that the Scriptures become intelligible. Paul was sure that this was true of the Old Testament. In II Corinthians 3:15-16 he describes the inability of the Jews to understand their Scriptures apart from faith in Jesus Christ. This is equally true of the New Testament. Apart from the acknowledgment of the Christ event, we cannot make sense out of the New Testament.

When we seek to describe the process by which the written Word was brought into being, we must begin with the revelation event. This is seen most clearly as we think of the New Testament. God comes to us in Jesus Christ. He reveals himself in the birth, the life, the teachings, the death, the resurrection, and the exaltation of Jesus Christ. The New Testament Church is the fellowship of those who, under the guidance of the Holy Spirit, have come to understand the significance of that which God has done for man in Jesus Christ. The revelation event calls into being the believing community. Then as the community seeks to give an account of itself to the world, it produces, under the guidance of the Holy Spirit, a literature in which it points beyond itself to the Christ event. In time this literature becomes collected into a Canon made up of books which the Church, under the guidance of the Spirit, has found to be true to the Church's understanding of the meaning of the coming of God in Christ. As heresy arises, this written Word becomes first the *norm* by which Christian preaching and teaching are tested, then, as the Church moves farther away from the Christ event, the written Word becomes the *source* to which the Church itself must go for knowledge of the message to be proclaimed. And as the Church moves into the centuries, the written Word becomes the *only* source of knowledge of the revelation event.

While this process is most easily traced in the development of the New Testament, a similar process can be seen in the production of the Old Testament. The People of God of the Old Testament are called into being by God's revelation of himself in certain events of their history, and the Old Testament is the literature through which the People of God set forth their understanding of the Covenant which God made with Israel.

But the written Word is never purely a record of past events. It points always beyond itself to the God who has come to us in Christ. It is the place at which God confronts us today. It is profitable for teaching, for reproof, for correction, for training in righteousness. The man of God who is deeply grounded in the Scriptures is prepared "for every good work."

PAUL'S FAREWELL MESSAGE

II Timothy 4:1-22

Timothy's Ministry (4:1-5)

The same three themes already noted in the third chapter and in the letter as a whole are mingled in a somewhat unorganized pattern in Paul's farewell message to Timothy. These are Paul's concern for the fidelity of Timothy, his personal testimony as an example to Timothy, and his warning against false teachers. They are the concerns of an old man, looking back upon his lifework as almost finished and forward to the life that lies beyond the grave.

The final charge to Timothy is given "in the presence of God and of Christ Jesus who is to judge the living and the dead." This description of Christ Jesus is incidental to the movement of the passage as a whole, but it does add urgency to the charge.

Christians are to live in this life as men who know that they must appear before the judgment seat of Christ to receive good or evil according to what they have done in the body (II Cor. 5:10).

Paul charges Timothy by Christ's "appearing and his kingdom." These ideas also strengthen the charge. They are particularly appropriate in connection with the reference to the work of Christ as the Judge of all mankind. The core of the charge is in the command, "Preach the word." By "the word" is meant the message of the gospel. Timothy is to proclaim the message which has been entrusted to him as a minister of the gospel of Jesus Christ, to announce that "God was in Christ reconciling the world to himself" (II Cor. 5:19). In proclaiming this message he is to speak with a tremendous sense of urgency, born of his understanding of the greatness of the salvation which God had provided in Jesus Christ and his knowledge of the need of man for this salvation. There must be about the proclamation of the gospel a sense of passion and of power, for the future is with the intense faiths.

In verses 3-4 the warning against false teaching appears again. But there is a new note here—that the false teachers arise because people demand them. The message of the gospel, if heard and understood, can be a source of comfort, but Jesus Christ confronts men as a Man of offense. He makes deep and searching demands of those who would follow him. Therefore, the message of the gospel wounds before it heals. Jesus can come as the great disturber of human life. And when the full offense of the gospel has been felt, there will always be those who want its message softened, so that it will not disturb them too deeply. There are times when the minister is tempted to play the role of protector for his people, shielding them from the full impact of the Word of God. Congregations will be tempted to "accumulate for themselves teachers to suit their own likings" and to "turn away from listening to the truth." Such congregations may be quite ready to substitute some popular "myths," which confirm them in their prejudices, for the unpopular truths which are rooted in a sound understanding of the Christian faith and which cut across their established customs. Verse 5 turns again to the charge to Timothy. He is to be always steady, ready to endure suffering and to do the work of an evangelist. If he does this, he will fulfill his ministry (see also Acts 20:24).

Paul's Departure (4:6-8)

Verses 6-8 include personal testimony from Paul. The first reference is to his death as a drink offering which is to be poured out (see Phil. 2:17), and the second to his death as a time to set sail and be with Christ (see Phil. 1:23). What were figures of speech in Philippians are now to become actual experience. Of course, death is not immediately at hand. Paul still hopes to live until Timothy comes to him. But he knows that he is very close to the end of the road. He can look back upon his earthly pilgrimage as finished. He has fought the good fight. In the great struggle between good and evil he has given the full impact of his mature life in the cause of Jesus Christ. Life in any event is a struggle. But it makes a lot of difference whether one fights on the right or the wrong side. Paul has finished his course. Underlying the passage as a whole there is the idea of a race that is to be run on a course that has been laid out by the Lord. Paul has kept the faith. He has remained consistently loyal to the great insights which have come to him from his Christian faith. His understanding of life has been tested at many places. But he has remained obedient to the heavenly vision which was given to him on the road to Damascus. He has given his life to testifying to Jews and Gentiles "that they should repent and turn to God and perform deeds worthy of their repentance" (Acts 26:20). As verse 7 looks back on life, verse 8 looks forward to the future, which for Paul is bright with hope. As the runner who has completed his course, he expects to receive from the Lord his reward, the crown of righteousness. This involves for him both acceptance with God and the experience of being "conformed to the image of his Son" (Rom. 8:29). This personal testimony becomes a message of hope for all true followers of the Christ when Paul declares that the Lord, the righteous Judge, will give the same crown of righteousness "to all who have loved his appearing."

Requests and Warnings (4:9-15)

These verses are filled with references to individuals, supplying interesting information on the character of the persons mentioned. Demas, in love with this present world, has deserted Paul and gone to Thessalonica. We wonder what sort of reception the deserter received among the Thessalonians. Others have left;

Luke alone is with him. The tribute to Mark implies that Mark has completely redeemed himself in Paul's opinion. There is a wealth of human interest in Paul's need of the old cloak left in Troas with Carpus, and in his yearning for the books "and above all the parchments." We wish we knew more about the way in which Alexander the coppersmith had wronged Paul. Certainly he had opposed Paul's message, and Paul sees fit to warn Timothy about him.

The Report of the First Defense (4:16-22)

Almost incidentally, Paul in his closing remarks gives us a report of a trial or hearing which he has recently had. He has been deserted by his friends from Asia. Evidently it was not safe for men to be known as friends of Paul in Rome at this time. Deserted of men, he has had in his trial a tremendous sense of the presence of the Lord. And he has used his trial as an opportunity of witnessing again to the Gentiles concerning Jesus as Lord and Savior. He has been saved "from the lion's mouth." This could be taken literally, for the Christians were often thrown to the lions, and Paul, in I Corinthians 15:32, refers to having "fought with beasts at Ephesus." But more probably it is a proverbial expression for being saved from great and imminent danger. This gives the setting for the final affirmation of faith. Paul is confident that the Lord will rescue him from every evil and will save him for his heavenly Kingdom. This does not mean that he expects to be delivered from death, for the whole passage shows that he knows that death is imminent. It does mean that from the many experiences of the saving power of the Lord in his earthly pilgrimage he has become confident that the Lord will not desert him in the hour of death and will preserve him for his Kingdom. The words confirm his testimony in verses 6-8 and come to each Christian as the basis for hope. As we fix our hope on the Lord as our personal Savior from sin and as the ground of our hope of eternal life, we can join with Paul when he says, "To him be the glory for ever and ever. Amen." And we also can receive Paul's benediction as he writes to Timothy: "The Lord be with your spirit. Grace be with you."

GREETINGS, INCLUDING A SUMMARY
OF THE GOSPEL

Titus 1:1-4

Acceptance of the Pauline authorship of the Letter to Titus
means that it must be placed between the first and second imprisonments in Rome, for Paul was obviously a free man when
he wrote. This will give a date between A.D. 64 and 66. It cannot be determined whether it was written before or after First
Timothy, but it must be placed before Second Timothy.

The letter is remarkable for a very long introduction, in which
appears one of the three great summaries of the gospel which
are the outstanding passages of this epistle. The other summaries are found in 2:11-14 and 3:4-7. The opening verses are
to be compared with Romans 1:1-7 and Galatians 1:1-5. This
involved introduction, unusual in a letter written to a friend,
indicates the intensity with which Paul seeks to set forth his
understanding of the gospel.

Paul begins by describing himself as a slave ("servant") of
God. The expression is unusual. In other places he has called
himself the slave of Christ (Rom. 1:1 and Phil. 1:1). He also
identifies himself as "an apostle of Jesus Christ." The original
meaning of "apostle" is "messenger." Paul knows that he has
been sent by Jesus Christ. The letter is addressed to Titus, but it
speaks, through Titus, to the Church at large. Paul has been sent
"to further the faith of God's elect and their knowledge of the
truth." "God's elect" are the Christian Church. This community
is present in the world because God has called it into being. It is
made up of those who have heard the gospel and have responded
to it. Paul's aim is to strengthen and deepen the convictions of
the believing community, to further the knowledge which these
Christians have of the truth. "Truth" can be defined as agreement with reality. Through the revelation which has come in
Jesus Christ we have true knowledge of God, of man, and of
human destiny. This knowledge makes for "godliness," that is,
for piety and for righteous living. Here is the unity of correct
knowledge and righteous living which is emphasized so strongly
throughout the Pastoral Epistles.

Eternal life, in this passage as in other places, means both a new quality of life in this world and the hope of the continuation and consummation of this kind of life after the crisis of death. God promised this eternal life "ages ago and at the proper time manifested [it] in his word." God never lies. He never deals in deceit. In this, God stands in sharp contrast to the Evil One, who is a liar from the beginning and the father of all lies (John 8:44). God's demand of truth is rooted in his own Being. Truth is something that we owe to God. Concern for loyalty to the truth which rises above all questions of expediency is at the heart of the Christian faith.

The promise of eternal life was made "ages ago." We cannot be sure whether Paul is referring to promises concerning the hope of eternal life made in time past to the fathers or to the divine intention at the creation of man to grant him eternal life. It is more logical to think of the former, for in this case we have a promise made and a promise kept. But in either case, God has seen fit at the proper time to give to man a manifestation of eternal life. Note the reference to "the proper time." The Christ event came at a time of God's own choosing (see also Gal. 4:4). Moreover, God manifested eternal life "in his word," that is, in the whole Christ event. It is there that God speaks to men in his Son.

Particular emphasis may be given to the revelation of the resurrection life which was given in the resurrection of Jesus Christ from the dead. It is through the resurrection of our Lord Jesus Christ that the believer's hope of eternal life becomes assured (I Peter 1:3-4). While the manifestation of eternal life is given in the Christ event, the knowledge of the significance of this event is made known through the proclamation of the gospel. Paul bears personal witness to the fact that he has been entrusted with this proclamation by the command of God (see also Gal. 1).

The letter is written to Titus, who is not mentioned in the narrative of Acts. Paul took Titus with him on the visit to Jerusalem described in the second chapter of the Letter to the Galatians. Titus went there as an example of a man who was fully accepted in the Christian community but who had not received the rite of circumcision. We would judge from this that he was a Greek and probably a convert of Paul's. Paul refers frequently to Titus in the Letters to the Corinthians. He sent him to the Corinthians to stimulate their interest in the offering which he

was taking for the suffering saints at Jerusalem. He commended
Titus to them as his partner and fellow worker. Here he calls
Titus his "true child in a common faith." When Paul writes this
letter he has left Titus in Crete. At the close of the letter he
asks him to join him at Nicopolis. When he writes Second Timothy he has sent Titus to Dalmatia (II Tim. 4:9).

INSTRUCTIONS FOR TITUS' MINISTRY IN CRETE

Titus 1:5—3:11

The Qualifications of Elders (1:5-9)

In verse 5 Paul instructs Titus to appoint "elders" (the Greek
word is "presbyters") in every town. And in verse 7, he proceeds
to set forth the qualifications of the "bishop." It is obvious that
he is talking about the same officer. The implications of this
passage are so clear that most students accept the identity of the
offices in the New Testament. Some make this admission but say
that the distinction between the two offices came after the time
of the writing of the New Testament.

Titus is left in Crete to set right the things that are defective.
He is expected to deal with false teachers and with inadequate
interpretations of the meaning of the gospel and to bring discipline to the church in Crete. He is given major responsibility for
appointing elders in every town. Since the method by which he
was to make these appointments is not described, it can be interpreted in terms of either a Presbyterian or an Episcopal understanding of Church government. We can be reasonably sure
that he ordained such elders in a public service which involved
the laying on of hands.

The qualifications of the elder as stated here should be compared with those given in I Timothy 3:1-7 (see comment). Certain things have been added here. Verse 6 is concerned for the
family life of the elder. He is to be judged in part by the success
which he has had in communicating the faith to his children. He
must understand that in his office he is God's steward, responsible to God for the way in which he bears himself. He must have
learned self-discipline. The man who cannot control himself is
not apt to be able to govern the church of God.

Verse 9 adds to the qualifications of elders as given in First Timothy: soundness in the faith, capacity to give instruction in sound doctrine, and ability to answer adequately those who speak against sound doctrine. These qualifications are implied if not actually stated in the letter to Timothy. The emphasis on them here is probably related to the situation which Titus faces in Crete, as set forth in the verses which follow.

Warning Against False Teachers (1:10-16)

The heresy with which Titus was to deal in Crete is not described in detail, but there are enough hints to give some idea of its nature. First, the leaders of this party within the Cretan church refuse to acknowledge the authority of Paul as an Apostle or of Titus as his messenger. Paul accuses them of being insubordinate men. Second, Paul is especially concerned with "the circumcision party." The heresy must have had Jewish roots. We would judge on the basis of verse 14 that the teaching of these men rooted in Jewish myths and that it involved a rejection of Paul's understanding of the gospel. The best guess is that here was a form of Christian piety in which an attempt was being made to fasten the legalism of Judaism, with its concern for ceremonial and ritual purity, on a portion of the Christian community. We would judge also that there was little relation between this religion of form and ceremony and righteous living. It is in his effort to combat this heresy that Paul writes the frequently quoted verse: "To the pure all things are pure, but to the corrupt and unbelieving nothing is pure; their very minds and consciences are corrupted" (vs. 15). The "pure" stand in contrast to the corrupt and unbelieving. Those who are marked by righteous living and sound faith need not be troubled by such things as laws of clean and unclean or degrees of ceremonial defilement. Jesus Christ has reminded his followers that they are defiled by the evil things which come out of the heart, not by the food they eat. Mark comments: "Thus he declared all foods clean" (Mark 7:19). Paul has been persuaded by the Lord Jesus that "nothing is unclean in itself" (Rom. 14:14). There is no religious value involved in abstinence from pork or abstinence from meat on Friday. Paul cut through every tendency to interpret religion in terms of dietary laws or ceremonial defilements when he wrote: "For the kingdom of God does not mean food and drink but righteousness and peace and joy in the

Holy Spirit; he who thus serves Christ is acceptable to God and approved by men" (Rom. 14:17). The other side of this truth is that nothing can be pure to those whose minds and consciences are corrupted. Such people are not fitted for any good deed. If we are living in rebellion against God, we cannot perform works that are acceptable with him. (Verse 15 is often cited as a statement of the way in which what we are determines what we find in others. It is true that we judge others against the background of our own inner life, and that we reveal ourselves in the things we see in others. But this idea is probably foreign to the thought of this verse.) In its essence, the Cretan heresy was probably the effort to substitute a religion of form and ceremony for a religion of commitment to the Lord Jesus Christ.

In verse 12 Paul quotes with approval a line from the Greek poet Epimenides, a poet and philosopher of Crete who lived about six hundred years before Paul. He quotes from a Greek writer, Menander, in I Corinthians 15:33 but does not identify the saying as a quotation. In Luke's report of Paul's speech on Mars' Hill there is a quotation from another Greek poet, Aratus (Acts 17:28). When we compare these three quotations with the way in which Paul's mind is saturated with the Old Testament (over eighty-eight quotations), we know that his roots are Jewish rather than Greek.

"Cretans are always liars, evil beasts, lazy gluttons," is the quotation from Epimenides. It illustrates the basic corruption of character faced by those who proclaimed the gospel in Crete. Paul faced a world in which "to play the Cretan" had come to mean "to play the cheat and liar" and "to play the Corinthian" meant "to play the prodigal and libertine." But in Crete, as in Corinth, the proclamation of the gospel could become the power of God unto salvation for those who believed.

Sound Teaching for Various Groups (2:1-10)

Against the background of the acknowledged corruption of Cretan life, Paul urges Titus to call his people to high standards of Christian living. It is unnecessary to comment in detail on the standards to be set for the various age groups. It is clear that the older women were to live in such a manner that they could train the younger married women and that Titus himself was to set an example for the younger men.

Verses 9-10 contain a special message to the slaves. Here

Paul assumes the institution of slavery as part of the structure of society in the ancient world. And he urges Christian slaves to bear themselves in the situation in which they are placed in such a manner that they may adorn the doctrine of God their Savior (see the comment on the Letter to Philemon).

A Second Summary of the Gospel (2:11-15)

The detailed instructions which Titus is to give to the various groups within the Christian community are not merely moral demands, set forth in isolation from the context of Christian thought and life. Christians are to look back to the grace of God which has been revealed in the Christ event and forward to the full revelation of the glory of Jesus Christ at his coming. They are to live in this present world as men who wait for the coming of their Lord. Both the backward look and the forward look are parts of the Christian motivation for righteous living.

The definite act of God in the past which is an expression of God's infinite grace includes the whole manifestation of the Son of God in the days of his flesh. This act of God is for the salvation of all men. Since this passage follows immediately after the message to the slaves, the reference may be first of all to men in all stations of life. The grace of God comes for the salvation of all men, regardless of their condition of life in this world. But we can be sure that Paul's thought included the universality of the gospel, in that its message was addressed on equal terms to Jews and Gentiles, to all men of all races and nations. The reference is, of course, to the saving purpose of God which reaches to all men. The witness to this saving grace of God has not yet been carried to all men. When Paul wrote, only a tiny fraction of the human race had received the message.

The effect of this manifestation of the grace of God is to lead men "to renounce irreligion and worldly passions, and to live sober, upright, and godly lives in this world." Implied here is the contrast between life in this world and life in the world to come, but it is "in this world" that believers are to renounce irreligion and worldly passions and live righteous lives. They are to do this as those who are awaiting the blessed hope, "the appearing of the glory of our great God and Savior Jesus Christ." As the margin of the Revised Standard Version shows, an alternate translation could be: "of the great God and our Savior." There is no vital doctrinal issue at stake, as the ascription of

deity to Jesus in the Pastoral Epistles is beyond dispute. But if
the Revised Standard Version translation is correct, this is a passage in which Jesus Christ is named as "our great God and
Savior." And the movement of the passage as a whole seems to
favor this translation. The reference is to the revelation of the
glory of Jesus Christ which will be given at his second coming.
While not stated here, a similar promise is given to all Christians who will, in the life beyond the grave, see their Lord face
to face.

Verse 14 defines what Christ has done for those who are his.
The One who gave himself for us has been named as our great
God and Savior. The Eternal Son, who is equal to the Eternal
Father in power and glory, gives himself for us. As Paul ex-
presses it elsewhere, "the Son of God . . . loved me and gave him-
self for me" (Gal. 2:20).

A twofold statement of the purpose of the death of the Son
of God is set forth. Jesus Christ gave himself for us "to redeem
us from all iniquity." The statement expresses the idea of deliverance. He who commits sin is the slave of sin (John 8:34).
But Jesus delivers us from the power of iniquity. This statement,
however, does not exhaust the purpose of God. Jesus gave himself for us "to purify for himself a people of his own who are
zealous for good deeds" (2:14). Redemption is followed by
sanctification. Christ seeks to purify a people who will be his
peculiar possession. The Church is the People of God, taking the
place of the Covenant people of the Old Testament as the instrument of God's redemptive purpose in the world. And the visible
symbol of the process by which these People of God are prepared for their destiny is that they are zealous for good works.
The redemptive act issues in the calling into being of a holy
people.

Some Marks of Christian Character (3:1-2)

At the heart of the preceding passage there is the great vision
of the Christian community, rooted in God's redemptive act in
the past and looking forward to the full revelation of the glory
of Jesus Christ. It is a community which has a strong consciousness of being the Lord's own people, the peculiar instrument of
his redemptive purpose for all mankind. But the members of
this believing community have to live in this present world. They
have to take their place in the political and economic order.

Titus, therefore, is to urge them to be submissive to rulers and authorities, and to be obedient to those who are over them. Nothing is said here of the limits of this obedience, but it would be understood that the Christians owed their first allegiance to Jesus as Lord (see Acts 5:29). They are to be "ready for any honest work." There is a consistent emphasis on the need for readiness to work within the Christian community. That they are to "speak evil of no one" does not forbid honest appraisal; it does forbid the needless spreading of evil reports. Christians are to show toward all men an attitude of gentleness and courtesy.

Some Marks of the Unregenerate Man (3:3)

The listing of some of the characteristics of Christian conduct prepares the way for an enumeration of some of the marks of the unregenerate man. The picture which is given here of man in sin is not a pleasant one, but it is a realistic portrayal of human society which has not been redeemed by the impact of the gospel. This verse, with its description of man's need of redemption, in turn prepares the way for the third statement of the nature of the gospel which Titus was to proclaim.

A Third Summary of the Gospel (3:4-7)

In these verses there is a great statement of the doctrine of justification by faith alone. The emphasis of the Pastoral Epistles is upon the unity of right thinking and right living, with constantly reiterated emphasis on the importance of good works. But these letters never fall into the legalism in which good works are made the basis of salvation.

This statement is similar to the other summaries of the gospel in this letter in that it looks backward to an event in which the goodness and kindness of God our Savior appeared. Again the implied reference is to the whole Christ event, including the birth, the life, the teachings, the death, the resurrection, and the exaltation of Jesus the Lord. It was in the coming of Christ that, in a distinctive way, the goodness and loving kindness of God our Savior appeared. The pronouns in the passage refer to God. It is God our Savior who reveals his goodness and loving kindness. It is God who saves us. It is God who pours out upon us his Holy Spirit.

To say that God "saved us" refers to God's action in sending his Son, and also to God's action as he lifts each individual sinner out of his lost condition and sets him in a new relation to himself. This saving act is not based on "deeds done by us in righteousness." God saved Saul of Tarsus when he was on his way to Damascus as the persecutor of the Church. He saved the Christians in Crete when they were living in the sins described in verse 3. He "shows his love for us in that while we were yet sinners Christ died for us" (Rom. 5:8). If God does not save us "because of deeds done by us in righteousness," what then is the basis of his saving action? Paul can only answer that God saves us "in virtue of his own mercy." In a sense this is not an answer, because it does not point to anything that we can do. It leaves the mystery of God's saving act in his own mercy. Beyond this we cannot go.

But in this passage Paul does set forth the way in which salvation comes to us. God saves us "by the washing of regeneration and renewal in the Holy Spirit." God saves us by the washing of regeneration. The reference to "washing of regeneration" is almost certainly to baptism as the act in which man responds to God's offer of salvation. In receiving baptism the believer acknowledges Jesus as Lord and identifies himself with the Christian community. In baptism the believer makes that confession of faith which the Lord demands of his followers. But we should not interpret the phrase in any way that would make regeneration through baptism artificial or magical. The necessity of public confession and public identification with the Christian community must be upheld as the response which God asks of us. But the experience of regeneration itself is a creative work of God, which man cannot manipulate. It is God who gives to the sinner a new heart and creates a new life within him.

God saves us by "renewal in the Holy Spirit." In this passage all three persons of the Godhead appear. If Jesus Christ is God manifest in the flesh, the Holy Spirit is God present with us in the Spirit. When God lifts us out of the state of sin and misery and sets us in a new relation to himself, he renews us in the Holy Spirit. The Spirit, "poured out upon us richly through Jesus Christ our Savior," applies to our hearts the redemption wrought out through Jesus Christ. The Spirit brings home to us the message of the gospel. The Spirit moves in our hearts prompting us to do good and enabling us to overcome the lusts of the flesh.

Believers are justified by God's grace. God freely pardons all of our sins and accepts us as righteous in his sight. In this experience, we become children of God. The Spirit witnesses in our heart that we are indeed children of God (Rom. 8:16). In the New Testament the idea of sonship is always associated with the thought of our inheritance as heirs of God. By the grace of God, we become heirs in the "hope of eternal life." The great summary of the gospel is commended as a saying that is "sure" (vs. 8a).

Final Injunctions (3:8-11)

In his final injunctions to Titus, Paul emphasizes three things. First, there is the necessary connection between saving faith and good works. The summary of the gospel in verses 4-7 gives a classic statement of the rejection of good works as a basis of salvation. This does not in any sense weaken the certainty that saving faith must be revealed in transformed life. Second, there is the warning to avoid needless controversy. The Pastoral Epistles give unqualified insistence on the necessity of preserving the faith in its purity; the believing community must at all costs hold to the true understanding of the meaning of what God has done for man in Jesus Christ. But Titus is warned against "stupid controversies, genealogies, dissensions, and quarrels over the law." Debates over such things are pronounced "unprofitable and futile." Third, there is the warning against men who are factious, that is, men who seek to destroy the unity of the Church. Such men are to be rebuked, and if the rebuke is not heeded, they are to be avoided.

Instructions and Greetings (3:12-15)

These verses imply that Paul was a free man, planning for the spread of the gospel in the Gentile world. He plans to send Artemas or Tychicus to Crete. His purpose was probably to relieve Titus temporarily of his duties in Crete and to make it possible for him to come to Paul. We know nothing of Artemas. Tychicus is well known as one of Paul's most trusted messengers. Since II Timothy 4:12 indicates that Paul sent him to Ephesus, the probability is that Artemas was sent to Crete. There were three places in the Roman Empire named Nicopolis; the reference here is probably to the Nicopolis on the western shore of Greece. We have no other reference to Zenas the lawyer, but Apollos is mentioned both in Acts and in the Epistles. When

Paul writes, Apollos and Zenas are in Crete on a preaching mission. There is a reminder of the need for Christian hospitality and for financial help for these men in their ministry of evangelism. The Christians in Crete are urged to do their part in helping these preachers and all others who are in urgent need. Readiness to give this kind of help is recognized as a good work, a sign of a Christian life which is not unfruitful.

Those who are with Paul join him in sending greetings. These greetings are sent to Titus and to all those "who love us in the faith." Paul speaks to them, and to all who will read this letter, when he says, "Grace be with you all."

THE LETTER OF PAUL TO

PHILEMON

INTRODUCTION

The Letter to Philemon is accepted by all as a genuine letter
from Paul. It was written, of course, with no thought of its ever
being preserved. When he wrote it Paul had no idea that it would
find a place in the writings that would become the Scriptures of
the Christian Church. The occasion that called forth this letter
was Paul's wish to plead with his friend Philemon for a runaway slave named Onesimus.

Philemon is not mentioned in any other place in the New
Testament. But Onesimus is referred to in the Letter to the Colossians as coming from Colossae (Col. 4:9), and Archippus, who
is mentioned in the greetings of this letter, is given a special
charge in the Letter to the Colossians (4:17). We should notice
also that the five Christians (Epaphras, Mark, Aristarchus, Demas, and Luke) who send greetings to Philemon are also mentioned in the close of the Letter to the Colossians. The two
letters, therefore, were probably written at the same time.

Paul is a prisoner as he writes the Letter to Philemon. While
some students associate the Letters to the Colossians and Philemon (and also the Letter to the Philippians) with an imprisonment which Paul may have had at Ephesus, the general consensus
places these letters in the first Roman imprisonment. This would
date them about A.D. 62 or 63—a little more than ten years after
the Letters to the Thessalonians.

The Letter to Philemon is a revealing document. Careful study
of the letter itself enables us to re-create the story of Paul's conversion of Philemon, probably during his ministry in Ephesus,
and to see in our imagination the meeting of Paul and Onesimus,
probably in Rome, which resulted in the conversion of Onesimus
and led to his decision to return to his master.

The letter throws light on the character of Paul. The man who
could pen the massive Letter to the Romans could also write

a personal letter to a friend, revealing his tact, his consideration for the feelings of others, his understanding of human relations, and his remarkable capacity for friendship.

As Paul sends the slave, Onesimus, back to his master, Philemon, we see Christianity in contact with the institution of slavery, accepting its outer form but undermining it with a new understanding of master and slave as brothers in Christ. And we can discern here the pattern for the movement of Christianity in the social order.

COMMENTARY

Greetings (Vss. 1-3)

Paul begins the Letter to Philemon by identifying himself as "a prisoner for Christ Jesus." He does not mention his apostleship, for the letter is a personal letter to a friend. He mentions his imprisonment four other times in this brief letter of twenty-five verses (vss. 9, 10, 13, and 23). Emphasis on his own condition as a prisoner is probably part of his appeal to Philemon for mercy for Onesimus. Philemon could hardly afford to refuse his request when Paul wrote as a prisoner. Paul refers to himself as a prisoner "for Christ Jesus." In verse 13 he speaks of his imprisonment "for the gospel." It was because of his fidelity to Christ Jesus that Paul was in prison. Although the place of Paul's imprisonment cannot be identified with certainty, various lines of evidence point to the first imprisonment at Rome. Paul includes Timothy as an author of the letter but does not mention him again.

The letter is addressed to Philemon, whom Paul calls his "beloved fellow worker." The character of Philemon is defined more fully in the prayer (vss. 4-7). He must have lived at Colossae, since Onesimus, his slave, was from Colossae (Col. 4:9). Verse 2 indicates that Philemon had a house large enough to be a meeting place for the Christians at Colossae. He was rich enough to own slaves. Inasmuch as Paul had never been at Colossae (Col. 2:1) the probability is that Philemon was converted during Paul's ministry at Ephesus. It may have been at this time that Paul and Philemon worked together in the proclamation of the gospel. The letter is addressed also to Apphia. The way in which she is mentioned would suggest that she is Philemon's wife. And we would guess that Archippus is their son. In the closing injunction of the Letter to the Colossians, Paul sends to Archippus the message: "See that you fulfil the ministry which you have received in the Lord" (Col. 4:17). In this letter Paul calls him his "fellow soldier." These references suggest that Archippus was ordained to the ministry and had worked closely with Paul as a good soldier of Jesus Christ. The letter, which is a personal note to Philemon, is also addressed to the Colossian Christians who are meeting in his home for worship.

Paul's Prayer for Philemon (Vss. 4-7)

The general movement of this passage, which is typical of Paul, is clear. He gives thanks for Philemon's ministry to the saints and prays that Philemon may grow in his knowledge of the spiritual blessings which are available in Christ Jesus. But it is typical of Paul to start with one idea and then to interrupt himself with other related ideas and finally to come back to his original idea.

Paul starts out by saying that he thanks God always when he remembers Philemon in his prayers. This is one of a number of places in which Paul refers to his custom of praying for others (see Rom. 1:8; I Cor. 1:4; Phil. 1:3; Col. 1:3; I Thess. 1:2; II Thess. 1:3). Paul gives thanks when he mentions Philemon in his prayers because he has heard of Philemon's love toward all the saints and of his love and faith toward Christ Jesus. The probability is that Paul's information concerning the faith and love of Philemon has come to him from Epaphras. We learn from Colossians 1:7-8 and 4:12-13 that Epaphras is the minister at Colossae who has come to Paul in Rome, apparently for advice on how to deal with the Colossian heresy. At the time of Paul's writing he is a prisoner with Paul at Rome. While Paul's main concern is the love of Philemon, expressed in his ministry to the saints, he knows that the ministry of love to others which Philemon has carried on has grown out of his faith and his love for Jesus Christ. Christian action roots in Christian conviction and in deep devotion to Jesus Christ. Paul's prayer is that Philemon's expression of his faith in a loving ministry to other Christians will lead him into the realization of the riches of grace which are available in Christ Jesus. The full knowledge of the deep things of God is a matter of the heart as well as the head. We must live our way into the matured knowledge of the good things which are to be found in Christ Jesus. Paul returns to his opening thought as he tells Philemon that he has derived much joy and comfort from his knowledge of the way in which Philemon has refreshed the hearts of the saints. The picture of Philemon here is interesting. He is obviously a man of some wealth, and he has used his wealth to minister to the needs of his brothers in Christ. And as he has given himself to this ministry he has been deepened in his own love of Christ, and his faith in Christ as his Lord and Savior has been strengthened.

Paul's Plea for Onesimus (Vss. 8-20)

This is the heart of the letter. Paul wants to ask Philemon for mercy for Onesimus. He does not intend to tell Philemon exactly what he must do, preferring to leave this to Philemon's own sense of what the situation requires. He hopes that Philemon will receive Onesimus as a brother in Christ. Paul seems to hint that he would be very much pleased if Philemon would see fit to send Onesimus back to Rome to continue his work there.

Verse 8 reveals Paul's sense of his authority as an Apostle of Christ. He feels that he has the authority to command and that, if he does, Philemon will have to obey. But he does not wish to use his authority thus. He wants Philemon to do voluntarily from love that which Paul thinks he ought to do. There are times when those who are in authority have to command, but they are always in a much stronger position when they can call forth the obedience that is given freely as an expression of love.

Verse 9 breaks the movement of the appeal by an expression in which Paul refers to himself as an ambassador and a prisoner for Christ Jesus. (The margin gives as an alternate reading for "ambassador" the phrase, "an old man." The two words are very similar in the Greek, but the reading "ambassador" is undoubtedly correct.)

Onesimus is first mentioned in verse 10. Paul calls him his "child," whose father he has become in his imprisonment. This means, of course, that Onesimus has become a Christian through the witness of Paul. Onesimus has grown in the Christian faith until Paul can think of him as his spiritual son. Onesimus as a child of God stands in strong contrast to Onesimus the runaway slave. The word "Onesimus" in the Greek means "useful," and there is a word-play on the name in verse 11. He who has been "useless" has now become "useful." At last, Onesimus is living up to his name. It does not take much imagination to go behind verse 12 to the scene in which Paul and Onesimus decided that Onesimus as a slave must go back to his master. It must have been a very hard decision both for Paul and for Onesimus. But the man who has given himself in full surrender to Jesus Christ must do what he can to make right the wrongs that are in his past.

Perhaps there did not enter into the thinking of either Paul or Onesimus at this time any basic consideration of whether slavery as a form of the economic order could be justified in the light of the Christian conscience. In the world in which they lived it was accepted as the normal pattern. Christianity came first as a message of individual redemption to each man in the situation in which he found himself. The Apostles consistently urged the Christians who were slaves to be obedient to their masters and to seek to bear themselves in such a way that they would adorn the doctrine of God their Savior (see Titus 2:9-10). The Apostles saw all of human life in this world in the light of the wonder of the resurrection world which they had seen in Jesus Christ. They were expecting the end of this present world and the disclosure of the new world of God in the near future. In such a situation, the orders of life in this world were to be tolerated as part of the God-given pattern of life in which each man was to seek to live as a Christian. Consider, from this point of view, I Corinthians 7:25-31.

Although Paul does not tell Philemon that if he is a Christian he must free his slaves, he does discern a providential ordering of human affairs in the separation of Onesimus from Philemon, which meant that Onesimus, through his contact with Paul, has become a Christian. Philemon now has Onesimus back "for ever." Earthly friendships become eternal if they are grounded in a common surrender to Jesus Christ. Moreover, Philemon now has Onesimus "no longer as a slave but . . . as a beloved brother." The sense of brotherhood in Christ binds Paul, Onesimus, and Philemon together in a relationship that is eternal.

This understanding of common brotherhood in Christ sets Onesimus in a new relation to Philemon. It involves a respect for the personality of Onesimus which cannot be destroyed by the master-slave relationship. Onesimus, as a slave who is also a brother in Christ, is given a new dignity in which his human rights cannot be violated. While Christianity did not at once destroy the institution of slavery, it did set both master and slave in a relationship to Christ as Savior and Lord. Consider from this point of view I Corinthians 7:17-24 and Colossians 3:22—4:1. The passage from Colossians was probably written at the same time as the Letter to Philemon.

It is proper to ask each man to try to be Christian in the actual situation which he faces in life. But the Christian conscience must also in time call in question the institutions of society which violate the rights of persons and which cannot be defended at the bar of God's justice. No one seriously defends the institution of slavery today. It has been weighed in the balances of God and found wanting. It cannot be harmonized with the demands of the Christian conscience.

In a similar way, the pattern of segregation is being called in question in society today. We cannot condemn as unchristian all of those who still remain within the thought forms of the past. But Christian conscience is being aroused to the violation of the rights of persons involved in a pattern of enforced segregation which is based on racial inheritance. And in future generations other aspects of our society will increasingly be called in question in the light of the insights of an aroused conscience.

In verses 17-20, Paul deals skillfully with a delicate matter. The probability is that Onesimus, at the time of his flight, had stolen from his master's purse. Paul bravely offers to repay any loss that Philemon has sustained. This is a noble gesture on the part of a prisoner, but Paul had ways of getting money when he needed it. Moreover, he probably did not expect to have to repay the money. He gave Philemon a good opportunity to refresh the heart of the imprisoned Apostle, even as he had refreshed the hearts of the saints at Colossae.

Concluding Remarks (Vss. 21-25)

The prospect of a visit from Paul strengthens his plea for mercy for Onesimus, and a gracious tribute is paid to Philemon's prayers for Paul's release. Aristarchus, who by this time had become one of the most trusted of Paul's associates, was a representative of the Thessalonian church (see Acts 19:29; 20·4; 27:2; and Col. 4:10). A fitting close to any writing is found in Paul's words to Philemon: "The grace of the Lord Jesus Christ be with your spirit."